Prov. 25:41

the Apple

A Woman's Battle Plan:
Overcoming Forbidden Fruit in Marriage

D0967574

Rachel D. Lyne

TRILOGY
PROFESSIONAL PUBLISHING MEETS POWERFUL PROMOTION

A wholly owned subsidiary of TBN

The Apple

Trilogy Christian Publishers A Wholly Owned Subsidiary of Trinity Broadcasting Network

2442 Michelle Drive Tustin, CA 92780

Copyright © 2021 by Rachel D. Lyne

All Bible quotations, except those noted otherwise, are taken from the English Standard Version. The Holy Bible, English Standard Version. ESV® Text Edition: 2016. Copyright © 2001 by Crossway Bibles, a publishing ministry of Good News Publishers.

Scripture quotations marked NIV are taken from the Holy Bible, New International Version®, NIV®. Copyright © 1973, 1978, 1984, 2011 by Biblica, Inc.™ Used by permission of Zondervan. All rights reserved worldwide. www.zondervan.comThe "NIV" and "New International Version" are trademarks registered in the United States Patent and Trademark Office by Biblica, Inc.™

Author Photo Credit: Juliana Lane

No part of this book may be reproduced, stored in a retrieval system, or transmitted by any means without written permission from the author. All rights reserved. Printed in the USA.

Rights Department, 2442 Michelle Drive, Tustin, CA 92780.

Trilogy Christian Publishing/TBN and colophon are trademarks of Trinity Broadcasting Network.

For information about special discounts for bulk purchases, please contact Trilogy Christian Publishing.

Trilogy Disclaimer: The views and content expressed in this book are those of the author and may not necessarily reflect the views and doctrine of Trilogy Christian Publishing or the Trinity Broadcasting Network.

Manufactured in the United States of America

10 9 8 7 6 5 4 3 2 1

Library of Congress Cataloging-in-Publication Data is available.

ISBN: 978-1-63769-286-8

E-ISBN: 978-1-63769-287-5

Dedication

To my first true love, my Lord and Savior, Jesus Christ, who gently takes my hand and shows me the way of life in love. Without God's mercy, faithfulness, and nurturing care, I could not have imagined the blessings in store for me through trials. Without the Holy Spirit working through my raw and real prayers, I would be a hopeless woman, wife, and mother scrounging for meaning. Without the sacrifice of God's own Son, Jesus Christ, I would have no basis to claim hope, or joy, or peace, or victory! Every word in this book is dedicated to the blessed Three in One.

Acknowledgments

First and foremost, I humbly thank the Lord for His mercy and grace throughout the entire process of *The Apple*. Christ knows my heart more than any other human could imagine to.

An outpouring of thanks to my husband, who pushed past temptations and lies that the world tried to whisper and refocused his life to love his wife and children in the strength of Christ. He daily strives to protect, care for, and love his family despite the trials that came (and will come) our way. Brandon, thank you for being patient with me during the moments I forgot that you are a gift from God. You are a priceless treasure that I have learned to be forever thankful for.

My precious children. Though you were young during the years of testing that birthed this book, you unswervingly loved me despite my shortcomings and gave me a reason to go on. You have become my very best little friends. Though I humanly failed you at times, I pray that you see your mother as an overcomer—one who sacrificed daily for you to know that you are priceless and purposefully created by your Intelligent Designer who knew you before the beginning of time.

Special thanks to my God-fearing parents, the Rev. and Mrs. D, who I called upon many times for Scripture references. My mother sacrificed countless ways to support this calling upon my life. Mama, you are the most wonderful encourager, spiritual example, faithful woman, and loving friend that a daughter could have. Dad, thank you for being not only my father but my faithful pastor.

Thanks to my local Pennsylvania church family (who supported me during times of famine and times of plenty), the Minnichs (who listened to the Spirit by supporting me and my husband during our darkest moments), my friends (from all walks of life and beliefs), my local writing critique group (who helped me become the writer I am today), and my extended family (legacy and family is so important to my journey). Also, if it weren't for my fellow "Rachel" cousin nudging me toward publication, this book would not be in your hands today. To my Account Executive, Shelbi, the TBN family, and Trilogy Publishing for their steadfastness in prayer, abundance of encouragement, and heaven-centered vision. Thank you, everyone. May God bless you all in His glorious ways.

Thank you, dear Reader. Thank you for choosing to come here to seek guidance, help, freedom, and victory in your marriage and life. Perhaps you're broken, feeling defeated, or on your last thread of hope. This book was written for wives just like you. Sisters just like you. Daughters just like you. You're at the right place. Welcome.

Table of Contents

This book is made up of six segments, which sections the journey into manageable steps. Each section is purposefully placed, so please read the chapters in order. There is no "easy fix" or "shortcut" on this journey.

Wise words: Matthew 7:13-14; 13:18-23.

Preface

The Apple was penned during and after grueling battles against forbidden fruit in my life: unhealthy emotional attachment (EA) outside of the bounds of marriage. This book is a testament and standing truth of God's goodness when we humble ourselves. It is a sacrificial offering to the One who sacrificed so much to save me. The purpose of *The Apple* is to point all wives to truth in the Word of God, which leads to freedom according to His will.

This book was not written from the perspective of "Johnny and Susie" or someone who never experienced an EA's power and reality. During our time together, you won't be inundated with or bogged down by others' stories and circumstances. Yes, there are times in this book that I'm compelled to share my own battles and triumphs with you as a fellow sister who struggled with something that's common to us. However, this book isn't about my story—it's about the story told from creation that affects wives (and *all* women) today.

- The majority of *The Apple* was penned during my EA, while I was in the trenches. Emotions were high and the hurt needed immediate healing. Being in that dark place allowed *The Apple* to be relatable.

Despite the demands of everyday life and being trapped in an EA, I knew God's purpose for me was far greater than my faults (such is your purpose!).

- This book took me over a decade to write, and in that decade, technology boomed. I have confidence now that I didn't have 10 years ago, because, in that span, the Lord revealed to me how technology influences wives today. It's important to present this to you with relevancy to our times, shedding light on the evolving methods of the enemy.

Everyone, of course, has their own unique story and forbidden fruit that they fall prey to. Not everything here will resonate in your specific situation, but there is full confidence that God's Word won't return to Him void (Isaiah 55:11).

The Apple is a spiritual battle plan against EAs that has been carefully formulated by my experiences and from the Word of God for women. . . for you. Why? Because ladies, we are in constant spiritual warfare. A sleeping, apathetic, bitter Christian is easy prey on the spiritual battlefield.

Even though this book can be relatable to unmarried women, the main intent of this book is to sound the warrior call for wives who desire to battle the forces that seek to overtake their marriage and family. We must guard against EAs, and not only that, we must actively fight against and win over the temptations that can ensnare us. God wants His daughters to suit up and battle the darkness. Therefore, sisters, let's be a generation of "Warrior Wives," as I call us, who are conquerors, disciples, and leaders who bring other women to healing and victory through Jesus Christ.

Introduction

Preparation & Path

Letters. Words. Phrases. Sentences. Paragraphs. Language.

Humans communicate. We're relational creatures made by a relational Creator. Communication is a basic human function, yet words have the complexity to either breathe life or damage.

You are here for a reason. You are here because of words. Someone spoke life and love into your heart. Yet, in hearing that "still, small voice" in the deepest parts of your being, you know the words of that someone cannot be of God. You are here because you walked into the maze of beautifully disguised deceit, and you don't know if there is a way out.

You are not ignorant to "the apple" of emotional attachment outside of marriage—you know it's there. It tempted you. You thought about it. You saw it was pleasing. Perhaps you tasted it and you feel mystified or trapped in your choice. Now, you know what happens next. You're here because you know the result of tasting the forbidden fruit . . . and you desperately want to be free.

Beloved sisters, you're not alone on this road. It's a dangerous journey you're on, overrun with fear, darkness, and uncertainty. However, with God's direction, His Word, and support from those who have also traveled this road, you can overcome and end in victory in Jesus' name. You're encouraged to pay close attention to the forthcoming words, which were written as a map to help show you the path from your confusion and hurt to God's heart.

In all honesty ladies, when we are still consuming the apple (interesting turn of events when we realize that the apple consumes us!), we usually don't want to hear about God or His Word. During the EA, I was reluctant, at first, to accept that I was falling for the trap of the forbidden fruit— even defensive that I could possibly be in the wrong. Are you there today?

I like how Timothy Keller puts it: "The sin that is most destructive in your life right now is the one you are most defensive about."[1] Was I defensive when my husband would confront me or when the Spirit stirred within me, telling me I was wrong? I regret to say . . . absolutely.

It's not easy to resist the combative voices in our heads: from the world and from the enemy, which drown out the voice of God. Even so, reach deep inside you in this moment and remember truth: You can trust God's promises. You can lean on His Word. God knows you intimately—much more than any human could ever attempt or pretend to. Take heart in this moment. And take the hand of the Savior. Let Him lead you to His truth, which leads to lasting freedom.

It's important to note that this was written from the perspective of our role as Christian wives. If you're reading this book and you do not have a saving knowledge of the Lord Jesus Christ, please seek out a Bible-believing church and pastor for guidance into everlasting life (Romans 3:23; 6:23; 5:8; 10:9-10). When you clearly understand your Creator and how much He loves you, the once-dulled meanings of joy, peace, love, and hope gloriously come to life.

If your husband or the EA is physically abusive, seek immediate help through a counselor, medical/law enforcement personnel, your church, or crisis response organizations. If you're reading this book and are unmarried (dating, single, engaged, etc.), keep these words close with the intention of equipping your heart against the enemy in your future relationship.

How to Use This Book
Encouragement & Equipment

Note: When you see "EA" used, it can mean the emotional attachment itself or it can also represent the person involved in the emotional attachment, depending on the context.

Journaling

At key points, there are opportunities for you to *journal* on the pages provided for you in the back of this book. You may use another notebook or journal of your choosing. Take advantage of the journaling moments because it's the map of your journey, and it . . .

1. allows you to take time to reflect on what you read by writing down your current thoughts, emotions, and reactions, being honest with God and yourself
2. gives tangibility to the very real spiritual battle at-hand
3. sheds light on internal or outward areas in your life that may need to be uprooted or planted
4. spurns you to action by writing a personal battle plan against the enemy of your soul
5. is an expressive way to be creative in your

communication with God so you can freely pour out your heart instead of harmfully bottling emotions or thoughts

Once this book is complete, keep your journal. Maybe it will be an eye-opener for your spouse to see how serious you are about your marriage. Maybe it will be for your children to read about God's faithfulness someday. Maybe portions of it will help a friend in need when they are going through a dark time in their own marriage.

Most importantly, the journaling is for you. It will help you see how far you've come in your journey, how God provided, and how God answered when you were real and humble before Him. Having the journal is a tangible reminder of God's faithfulness, forgiveness, and love. Just as the Israelites had holidays, symbols, and documents to help them remember God's faithfulness, your journal will be there for you in the future to comfort you . . . especially if you find yourself in a maze once more.

Scriptures

"The study of God's Word for the purpose of discovering God's will is the secret discipline which has formed the greatest characters." —James W. Alexander

This warrior guide is extensively saturated with Scripture. You'll need to keep your copy of the Word of God handy throughout this book. All Bible quotations, except those noted otherwise, are taken from the English Standard Version. Scriptures are often listed for you instead of spelled out. I call them "Scripture Sprints." This gives you a great opportunity to research, stirring a passion within you to study the Word of God and not simply taking my word for it.

When we focus on God's Word, it:
1. Keeps our way pure
2. Helps us follow God's commandments
3. Guards us so we might not sin against Him

This is fleshed out in Psalm 119:9-11: "How can a young man (*or woman*!) keep his way pure? By guarding it according to Your Word. With my whole heart I seek You; let me not wander from Your commandments! I have stored up Your Word in my heart, that I might not sin against You" (emphasis added).

If Scripture Sprints appear, I urge you to open your Bible and read. They are there for your encouragement and benefit. The Sword is there. It's up to you to wield it.

Quotes

Throughout this book, you'll find quotes from various voices throughout history. I believe in the truth of the Bible and nothing but the Bible. So, when I choose a quote to include, I ensure it is Biblically sound. Some iconic names are quoted, and not all of those individuals, I realize, are looked upon with 100% favor by everyone for one reason or another. I don't choose a quote based on the human (every human is fallible). I choose quotes based off the inspired, infallible Word of God. I recognize that God can speak through whomever He wants to speak through in order to encourage and edify the body of Christ. 2 Timothy 2:14-26.

Prayer

Before you read another sentence, pray. Stop what you are doing and ask God to open your eyes and heart to the things He desires to reveal to you. Be vulnerable in your prayer and open up to the Holy Spirit. It's the first step to overcoming.

Don't know where to start? Pray against: a closed mind/ heart, bitterness, anger, hopelessness, fear, confusion, needless shame. Pray for: peace, understanding, forgiveness, openness, courage, love, surrender, and restoration. *Journal* your prayer.

What you're about to read in this book is spiritual and goes against our innate human nature. Our spiritual enemy will attack you, as the reader, just as he attacked me, the writer.

Therefore, know that I am praying for you. My prayer for you is that walls that were either meticulously or unknowingly built in your heart against what God intends for good would be recognized and dealt with by the fear of the Lord and His perfect love. That your thirst for truth is never sated. That you don't compare yourself with anyone but, in the same breath, recognize that you're not alone. That the enemy will not cloud your heart or mind and that God will shine the light so desperately needed in our world, lives, and hearts. That you feel His presence through His Word and come to the place of peace that you have so desperately longed for (Philippians 4:6-7). I also pray that the Lord be patient and merciful as you battle.

Now, with humble hearts and open minds, let's unearth the power of the Word of God and the Holy Spirit to change your situation into a story of triumph for His glory.

Section 1:
At the Ready

Intro

You've reached the first step in this book toward your destination of freedom in Christ from what binds you. The snare of emotional attachments/affairs can be suffocating, but there is hope. Cling to that hope as we take our first step in uncovering what God's Word has to say about your situation. I am so thankful that we have a God who knows us and knew our situation even before we took our first breath.

"A" is for Apple

WHY IS THE APPLE ENTICING?

Why call this book *The Apple?* Traditionally, the first temptation is depicted as an apple, even though it's described in the Bible as simply "fruit." The label of this book was intentional on a deeper level. The first thing we learn in grade school is, *"a" is for apple.* Subsequently, it's imperative to recognize the first temptation that led to the first sin in the first book of the Bible.

Genesis chapter three discusses "The Fall of Man" (and woman) in detail. Most everyone knows the account of Adam and Eve and roll their eyes. They've "heard it a million times" and may even doubt its 21st century relevancy. But do they really see what God intended through this introduction to the entire Bible? "Genesis" generally means the start or the beginning. Yet, I took particular interest in a synonym for Genesis—the "root": where something begins. It all began with a seed that sprouted roots, giving birth to the tree. And, just as Eve in the garden, we choose the fruit we will eat (and produce). Daily.

Which fruit from which tree will you eat? The ones intended for us or the one forbidden? For a classic reference, it sounds like *The Matrix* blue pill/red pill scenario, doesn't it? Eat the forbidden apple and know what's good and evil. Eat the fruit freely provided and continue in God's intended place of paradise. More often than not, as humans, we choose the former. But why?

The fruit itself wasn't evil. God's perfect fruit from the tree of the knowledge of good and evil was created by Him. Not for us to stumble, but to give humanity a choice. Eve had a choice, as we have a choice today. I challenge you to look beyond the result of that choice and analyze how she got to that place of decision. Because, ladies, we make these difficult decisions every day.

Let's dissect this passage into terms that you can hold on

to today. The first reason we choose the wrong fruit is . . . words. Surprising? Check out Genesis 3:1-5. The enemy of Eve's soul has a conversation with her. It's not a conversation of anger or hate. It's a conversation of compromise. The enemy offered another idea and a way other than God's intended way. And when those words reached her mind, they set a villainous trap.

The Apostle Paul, in 2 Corinthians 11:3, writes, "But I am afraid that as the serpent deceived Eve by his cunning, your *thoughts* will be led astray from a sincere and pure devotion to Christ" (emphasis added). The words of the serpent got to Eve. She dwelled on them. How do I know this? We witness her inner dialogue in Genesis 3:6:

1. She saw that the tree was good for food.
2. She saw it was a delight to the eyes.
3. She saw that the tree was desired to make one wise.

The action came after these three things were satisfied in her thought processes. Not surprisingly, these three phases apply to us today. They're what we consider first in our minds before acting upon a decision. The journey of sin is through the eyes of our mind first, then our physical eyes, then . . . the desire in our heart.

In today's terms, here are some parallels on how her choice to eat the fruit relates to us:

- The tree was good for food: The physical, practical, or even financial appeal. Maybe he's **rich**. He has a lot of money that you know you and your husband could never make in a lifetime. You crave that financial security. *Flip it* . . . Or, he's dirt poor and you admire how he can survive so meagerly, wondering to yourself if you could one day improve his situation.

- A delight to the eyes: The relational, sexual, or emotional appeal. Maybe he's **handsome**. Over the years, maybe the face of your spouse has become mundane and a new look and mystique excites you. *Flip it* . . . Or, maybe he's a touch on the homely side and your heart wants to show him how someone can love him.

- Desired to make one wise: The intellectual appeal. Maybe he's **smart**. He opens your mind to new worlds and makes you see things in a different light. But wait . . . isn't that what the enemy of our souls tried to pull with Eve? *Flip it* . . . Or, maybe he's not the sharpest tool in the shed and you feel a sense of accomplishment when you are the intellectual one "helping" him.

The trifecta of a perfect man society feeds us with is "smart, rich, and handsome." Think about that for a second. The world already knows what we are susceptible to and exploits it.

Now consider this: When you chose your husband, was he smart, rich, *and* handsome? Chances are, probably not 100%. You loved him despite his shortcomings. He knew your flaws and still said, "I do." You both smiled on your wedding day with anticipation, knowing even then that life wasn't going to be perfect.

When we engage in the forbidden fruit of an EA, it's not usually an immediate reaction to the invading thoughts. It's a slow compromise. For instance, we didn't accept someone other than our husband because that person spoke harshly to us or abused us. It's an easy compromise when someone swoons us with words we long to hear, words that our spouses may have stopped saying long ago.

With that in mind, look back up at the bullet points. Did you notice that the first example in each of the three points stems from worldly "needs?" Did you notice that the second examples (the *flip its*) also point to worldly "needs?" *Wait, what? I thought I would be helping someone! Isn't loving the unlovable a Godly thing to do—what a Christian would do?*

In being "selfless" and acting in "love" toward the EA, we may think we could gain the favor of God, since God is love, right? My friend, that would only twist the intended meaning of love and marriage, just as the enemy in the garden twisted the meaning of being like God.

The times we feel we're being selfless toward our EA are the moments we are truly selfish. Before you recoil at those words, I need to remind you that this writer, woman, wife, and mom believed the same lie that I was being selfless. There is a love from God and a healthy love for one another. However, there is a sin-zone beyond God's intended love, including all variations of "lust." Love is *never* a banner to hold high if we are openly entertaining the antithesis. Take a breath. Let's continue.

To explain the same result with a different perspective, consider this: Each time we think we're improving the EA's situation, we gain their favor, and it fills our own depleted worth-tank (especially if our marriage spurns feelings of unworthiness).

How many storylines in movies, books, and other media have the "boy meets girl . . . girl changes boy . . . girl makes boy a better person . . . they live happily ever after. The end." This storyline is used so many times because it's enticing, isn't it? I get it. That, my sisters, is why this trap of the enemy is so alluring. Being a "safe place" or "filling the gaps" for someone is appealing and gives us a sense of self-worth.

However, I challenge you to read Acts 20:24 and Luke 9:23. We need to set our sights on Jesus Christ and how He gives us worth. We need to remember Christ *because* the apple is real. For you. For me. For all generations before us. For generations after us, until the trumpet calls us home. The enemy has known humanity's struggle since day one. He knows our weaknesses. To combat temptations, we need to know our true adversary. Greater still, we need to know how to equip our minds and hearts. Even greater still, we need to know that the result of humility and obedience is victory. There is hope. There is an abundant life waiting for you if you choose to follow the love letter that God Himself wrote to you. Let's journey on.

Purpose & Plan

WHY SHOULD I FIGHT AGAINST THE ENEMY?

"You cannot know the will of God apart from the Word of God." —Former Washington Bible College President, Mr. George Miles

Hope. What a beautifully woven and intricate word. Hope is one of the most valuable things we can possess as humans (1 Corinthians 13:13). When we see ourselves or others lose that hope, we see catastrophic results. Decisions can be made out of desperation, apathy, or rebellion. We begin to lose sight of how God sees us and we minimize our importance.

Faith, hope, and love—these are connected to one another. I have witnessed instances that when hope waned, faith followed and, eventually, hearts turned to stone. If we lose all three, we lose our sense of purpose and being. We become callous to everything good the Lord has for us. Do your find yourself there today? If so, there is good news: the

Lord can soften hearts. As He told the Israelites in Ezekiel 36:26, He is capable of replacing our stone hearts with hearts of flesh.

Hope doesn't have to fade. There's a purpose for you. There's a plan for you. There's a purpose and plan for your marriage as well. God can still use you and your situation for His glory. Allow Him to. Let's strive to live in such a way that when God calls us home, our legacy produces ripple effects of His testimony.

I am here today because I had nearly lost all hope, but when the scales were taken off my eyes, I remembered that God *is* our hope. If it weren't for Jesus and His sacrifice, we would have no basis to hope! He is our reason to hope *and* the hope that will lead us safely Home. That realization and peace surged in and through me. It's such a relief to know that our purpose and plan is not our own but God's. That, my friend, is what I want you to see and experience in your own life!

Take this time now to pray and openly tell God how and why you may have lost hope. Then, ask Him to renew that spark within your heart to do His will. *Journal* about it.

God sees your situation (Matthew 10:29-31). One of the names of God is "El Roi," which means "the God who sees me." It was used by Hagar when she was in the throes of emotional pain. God saw her, heard her, and spoke to her (Genesis 16). Maybe you've cried for rescue many nights and days like I did.

Breathe. Read Mathew 11:28, "Come to me, all who labor and are heavy laden, and I will give you rest." Being involved in an EA zaps women of energy, hope, and so much more. When in that state, we may feel that God is distant, but we must trust that even though we might not feel God or see Him working, that He *is* working and always sees and hears us.

The Word of God in Proverbs 3:5-6 says, "Trust in the Lord with all your heart, and lean not on your own understanding; In all your ways acknowledge Him, and He shall direct your paths." This might be a life verse for some of you. It's a great Scripture to quote, but I want to make this clear and plain: We must acknowledge the Lord as God first in *all* our ways. To get back on the intended path for our lives, we need God's direction. And He will do it if we trust in Him, lean on His wisdom, and acknowledge Him in *all* our ways.

And, yup, you guessed it—that means no secret closets, habits, or relationships are to be kept from the Lord. "The end of the matter; all has been heard. Fear God and keep His commandments, for this is the whole duty of man. For God will bring every deed into judgment, with every secret thing, whether good or evil" (Ecclesiastes 12:13). A famous quote from Dr. Phil McGraw: "People who have nothing to hide, hide nothing." How freeing it would be if we had absolutely nothing to hide!

God wants you to be free. God is a jealous God and He not only wants the best for us, He wants *all* of us: our hearts, minds, and souls (Scripture Sprint: Luke10:27; Mark 12:30; Matthew 22:37; Deuteronomy 6:5; 10:12-13; 11:13-14; 13:3b; 30:6; Joshua 22:5).

That involves trust. Going back to Proverbs 3:5, "trust" can be defined as, "to believe, have faith, confidence and security in, to count on, or find refuge in." This is a foundation of faith—something we need to cling to!

If you've ever been rock climbing, you know the initial feeling of letting go of the rocks (or plastic knobs in my case!) when you're high up and relying on your belay to help you descend. It's such an unnatural feeling to just jump off with only a rope, isn't it? Countless times, I witnessed climbers freeze at the top, even though they're perfectly protected and safe to jump with the proper equipment. Our human instincts crave a tangible security sometimes. Therefore, know that the Lord will catch you if you take hold of the Word of God in this moment. It is our offensive weapon against the enemy (Ephesians 6:17) and a key to unlocking His purpose for you and your marriage. Let's not be stubborn or afraid, clinging to the surface of a mountain, but seek to understand what God's will is for us (Ephesians 5:17).

Let this psalm be your prayer as you seek to understand God's will: Psalm 25:4-5, "Make me to know Your ways, O Lord; teach me Your paths. Lead me in Your truth and teach me, for You are the God of my salvation; for You I wait all the day long."

Let the Lord lead. Your purpose is made perfect in Him.

And that's the truth!

Remembering God's truth will help you gain that faith, hope, and love back for the One who created you. For the One it was intended for. God promises never to leave us or forsake us. You can hope in Him. You can have faith in Him. You can love Him. And He has a purpose and a plan for *you*.

Read Titus 2:3-5. The relevancy is undeniable. If you don't own another goal for your life, may that one become paramount. We are to train others and to be examples and disciples to other women. What a beautiful purpose and aspiration!

Ladies, as Paul wrote to the Philippians in chapter one verse six, I write to you, "I am sure of this, that He who began a good work in you will bring it to completion at the day of Jesus Christ." You can be sure of the plan God has for you, too!

Section 2:
The Reality

Intro

These next four chapters are aimed straight at the heart of the matter—our own hearts. In this segment, we'll wrestle with fear, the consequences of actions, come face-to-face with what fruit we're bearing, and differentiate between light and dark. Some of these chapters may feel a bit uncomfortable, but soul-searching always is. Let's muster our fortitude and continue in hope, knowing what blessings await if we do not give up.

Fear & Faith

WHAT CAN STAND IN THE WAY OF VICTORY?

"Fear makes the wolf bigger than he is." — German Proverb

Fear is big in our culture. It's an even bigger concept in Christianity. The horrors of it and how to combat it are sung in worship songs, preached from the pulpit, and is the focus of many faith-filled books, blogs, and posts. Spiritual battles within and externally are largely preceded by fear.

It's no wonder anxiety is prevalent, depression lurks at every heart's doorstep, and we've become an increasingly isolated society. Fear can grip us tight, and it attempts to squeeze the last bit of enjoyable life from us. It affects our way of living: our attitudes, our words, our physical bodies, our minds, and our hearts.

Even when we've experienced past victories that sparked courage within, we sometimes crumble when fear invades once more.

Has your EA evolved from a forbidden place of hiding to needing to hide from it? Both stages of hiding cultivate anxiety, depression, and fear that wracks our souls. What happens when he saved your angry words about your husband that you regret? What happens when he is your kids' coach and knows all the parents? What happens when social media turns into a breeding ground of petrifying obsession, wondering if he will post pictures of you that no one else should see? What happens when he's a strong voice in your church? What happens when he follows half of your followers on Instagram? The enemy knows the tools to keep us locked up in fear, and much to everyone's chagrin, the largest and most accessible of those tools in our culture is technology. As of October 2020, 4.66 billion people in the world had access to the internet, with personal mobile devices accounting for 91% of the 4.66 billion internet users.[2]

Consider every app on your phone. Chances are the majority of those house the capabilities to make unhealthy emotional connections that damage marriages. The avenues of enemy penetration through technology are literally limitless and cannot possibly be encompassed in this book.

The words above may have struck a chord with you. Fear resonates. So, in this moment, stop reading, close your eyes, and take a breath . . .

****

Pastor Steven Furtick of Elevation Church from his dynamic "When Anxiety Attacks" sermon said, "The enemies that you fear today will be your testimony of triumph in your tomorrow."[3] Do you believe that? I certainly do . . . because I lived it. Was I afraid to take steps to cut ties with the EA and heal my marriage? Yes. However, I knew deep down that God would not abandon me in my efforts; I had to push past the fear in faith to reach triumph in Christ.

Take some time to research how God's chosen people battled and won against the enemies that were put in front of them; despite fear, they conquered and showed God's glory. God wants *you* to battle and endure in order to show the world His glory through your situation.

Knowing that God wants us to persevere, fear doesn't need to rule our lives. It doesn't define us. Speaking of definition, did you know that the word "fear" is both a noun and a verb?

It is considered a "thing" *and* an "action" (manifestation of feelings). Now, in your favorite search engine type "faith" or "definition of faith." You'll find it's only a noun! Interesting, right? We can act out our faith, yes, but *journal* about why you think it being a noun may be significant. In my mind, knowing how fear is diversely defined, it makes fear all the more dangerous as it grips my emotions and also my actions. I am encouraged, however, that faith is a noun—something I can wield against fear!

The word "fear" and its forms are used over 450 times in the New King James Version of the Bible. "Faith" and its forms are just shy of 400 appearances. Why is this? Because, simply put, fear can mean to be afraid of or to be in awe of something.

Do you fear man, or do you have a reverent fear of God?

Exodus 20:20 uses both forms of fear for a reason: "Moses said to the people, 'Do not fear, for God has come to test you, that the fear of Him may be before you, that you may not sin.'" This text tells us not to fear (be afraid) and clearly states that through testing, we understand how to fear (be in awe of) the Lord, which will ultimately keep us from sin.

Part of the reason you may be reading this book (and a reason why I wrote it) is because you have a healthy fear of the Lord, His power, and righteousness (1 Corinthians 4:2-5; Hebrews 10:26-27).

So, let's shift that tangible fear (noun) into an action fear (verb) of the Most High.

1 Peter 3:13 says, "Now who is there to harm you if you are zealous for what is good?" In the next passages in 1 Peter chapter three, it says, "But even if you should suffer for righteousness' sake, you will be blessed. Have *no fear* of them, nor be troubled, but in your hearts honor Christ the Lord as holy…" (emphasis added). We don't have to be afraid of man (Psalm 56:11)! We need to focus our eyes on Christ. Easier said than done, right?

The most comforting verses in the Bible that calm my fears come from Exodus 14:13-14, "And Moses said to the people, 'Fear not, stand firm, and see the salvation (*deliverance* in the original Hebrew) of the Lord, which He will work for you today. For the Egyptians whom you see today, you shall never see again. The Lord will fight for you, and you only have to be silent'" (clarification added).

Isn't it a great relief to know that God fights our battles? In many ways, it takes great anxiety away, doesn't it? Sister, don't forfeit the battle in loss at the cruel feet of fear.

Those verses in Exodus were commands from Moses:

> Don't fear.
> Stand firm.
> See the Lord's salvation/deliverance.
> Be silent/still.

The Lord's command in Isaiah 41:10 is similar: "Fear not, for I am with you; be not dismayed for I am your God…" and it comes with glorious promises (vv. 10, 13): "I will strengthen you, I will help you, I will uphold you with My righteous right hand…For I, the Lord your God, hold your right hand; it is I who say to you, 'Fear not, I am the One who helps you.'"

If you rely on the Lord's power in your life, you will see victory. Step out of your fear. Step into His goodness. Read Romans 8:15-17 and Psalm 16:8 for an extra dose of comfort.

A word of caution: "relying" does not mean that we hide ourselves away and bury our heads in the sand. Faith is active believing, not hiding. To illustrate, consider the depiction of an ostrich with its head buried in the sand. The jury is out on why or even if it does, but it's an interesting metaphor, nonetheless. It's traditionally assumed that they do this to escape stressful situations out of fear. Are you comfortably burying your head in the sand to avoid what's necessary for healing? The breakdown below of what I call "The Ostrich Principle," poses questions to help you discover if you are.

The Ostrich Principle:

- How – (Attitude) How am I approaching my situation? Hostile or humble? Am I resisting or am I conquering for Christ?
- Who – (Motive) Who am I pushing away? Who am I allowing to lead? Who am I trying to please?

- What – (Action) What happens when I bury my head in the sand and ignore my responsibility to act in faith? What does it solve if I'm sedentary in my resolve?

- When – (Situation) Am I involved in an EA due to an evolving situation in my life? Is it out of temporary convenience or during high tides of bitterness?

- Where – (Time/Place) Where am I giving my time? At the feet of Jesus or at the feet of fear? Where are the places I'm actively avoiding? Church? Am I neglecting time with friends who will point me to truth? Am I hiding from the spiritual battlefront during the call-to-arms?

- Why – (Thoughts) Why are there anxieties within me? Are they from burying my head in the sand? From ignoring warning signs from the Spirit?

Think on your answers and *journal* about them. If they are negative and fearful and don't revolve around answers pointing to Christ, do you feel shame or guilt? It's okay to feel the sting of these things (but not live there), because that means you are starting the journey of humility that leads to freedom. You are ready to hear the words written for you in the coming chapters.

The Apple

Cause & Consequences

WHAT HAPPENS WHEN I DON'T COMBAT THE ENEMY?

"A seed hidden in the heart of an apple is an orchard invisible." —Welsh Proverb

In the Garden, Eve didn't blame the fruit. She blamed the deceiver. Wouldn't it have been silly if she would've said, "Well, the apple was there, and it tempted me out of its beauty. It's the apple's fault for just being there for me to take." Sounds improbable, doesn't it? Interestingly enough, however, during the EA I was having, the EA said to me, "Sin? The apple made me do it." The EA said this either out of ignorance or as a blatant rejection of the reality of the deceiver, blaming sins on something other than his own decisions.

Don't we sometimes do the same thing, ladies? We blame our plight on sin nature, circumstances, or even our spouses. In doing so, we forget that there is an enemy of our very souls who works around the clock to capture our hearts. The blame will circle back to us. Sisters, we didn't fall because of the mere existence of the apple. We fell because someone spoke lies into our minds and hearts, resulting in idolization of and infatuation with the apple.

Initially, most of us may have disregarded the truth of the

consequences to feed our flesh's appetite.

But then, when we realize where our choices led us, we remember that there are always consequences to our actions. To believe otherwise is to deceive ourselves. We are not to be complacent about it. Causes and their respective consequences are alive and well.

And it's nothing new. Galatians 6:7-8 says, "Do not be deceived: God is not mocked, for whatever one sows, that will he also reap, for the one who sows to his own flesh will from the flesh reap corruption, but the one who sows to the Spirit will from the Spirit reap eternal life." That, my friends, is the ultimate example of cause and effect.

Another distinct example is found in Hosea 8:7, "For they sow the wind, and they shall reap the whirlwind." Is that true of your life today? Have you tried to grasp and cultivate what shouldn't be obtained and ended up in a whirlwind of confusion, fear, and pain? In the end, it ultimately causes destruction.

But praise be to God! Praise God that He makes a way. Praise God that He is Healer and Deliverer. Praise God that your situation doesn't define you. Praise God that your circumstance can be turned around for good when you humble yourself before Him and acknowledge that your choices may have led you far from Him.

Denial of sin and complacency about its consequences are toxic to our souls (Scripture Sprint: Ecclesiastes 12:14; Romans 2:6; Numbers 32:23; and Revelation 20:12-13 for a sobering reality check). We must deal with it firmly. Not confessing it will fester in our hearts, which is an effect that can be debilitating and terrifying.

But do not be afraid, friend. Psalm 103:9-11 is a great comfort: "He will not always chide, nor will He keep His anger forever. He does not deal with us according to our sins, nor repay us according to our iniquities. For as high as the heavens are above the earth, so great is His steadfast love toward *those who fear Him*" (emphasis added).

Ask yourself if your fear of man is more than your fear of God. To fear the Lord is to acknowledge His sovereignty, His judgement, and the consequences for your actions. We need to be careful to humble ourselves and follow His ways. It's a lot to take in, but time is short. Read Proverbs 9:10, then accept a hug of truth from Romans 8:31-39.

Now, read Ephesians 4:25-32. It's not all about fire, brimstone, anger, and judgement . . . we can grieve the Holy Spirit. We are capable of causing sadness to the One who comforts us in our time of need. On the next page is a chart of what things grieve Him and how to avoid them.

What Grieves the Holy Spirit	How to Avoid Grieving the Holy Spirit
Deception	Speak truthfully
Anger/rage that leads to sinning	Deal with it timely
Stealing (not just things or money, but time, affections, attention, etc.)	Work and relate honestly with the intention to share
Foul talk/slander	Uplifting words
Bitterness/resentment	Forgiveness
Clamor/verbal shouting	Kindness
Malice (ill will or evil intent)	Compassion

Looking at this chart, the left side occurred prevalently when I was involved in EAs. The right side was how I wanted to be treated and, over time, I realized that the right side was what was intended for my marriage. Even if the former foundation of your marriage has been cracked by the things that grieve the Holy Spirit, God gives us grace to build a foundation afresh that will withstand future storms. It's not too late for you. It's not too late for your marriage.

In Matthew chapter seven, you'll recall the parable of the foolish man who built his house on sand and the wise man who built his house on the rock. When the storms came, the house on the rock stood, and we all know what happened to the house on the sand. Now, let's look at this from a new perspective.

As Christians, we are always building. Metaphorical houses, perhaps, but always building. Now, I don't consider myself as having been a "fool," however, I now realize that I fooled myself into building my house on the sand. I know this because of the storms that occurred due to my EA. The storms made me realize:

1. What I was standing on was unsecure, shifting, and changing. Not just my situation, but my mood, thoughts, actions, and reactions. I was unstable.

2. I thought I thoroughly checked my foundation. But while in sin, I was blinded, and it wasn't as grounded in truth as I had believed it was. It was a cracked foundation.

3. "Building" my house was quick, easy, and cheap. The EA I had forged was an "easy" way out of my marital situation at first, but it quickly became more than I could handle.

4. The consequences came later during adversity (storms). During the storms, I was laden with anxiety, depression, and worry. When I was young and lived in Florida, we had to strap our home yearly to brace against real-life hurricanes. Being in the middle of many hurricanes both literally and figuratively, I know what that anxiety feels like when the sandy foundation isn't secure.

So, *journal* about or draw your current house. Where are you building it? What is the foundation like? Is there a storm wracking your home?

Now, consider this truth: The foundational and complete blueprint for marriage and home *is* the Word of God! Follow its direction, my friend. As it says in James 1:22, be doers of the Word and take action. I also caution you, sometimes we may need to rebuild our homes from the ground up. It takes time . . . and it's okay.

As you purpose to rebuild or repair your home to be on solid ground, read James 4:13-17. It speaks about how tomorrow is never promised (and many other passages). That passage is also a stark reminder that "whoever knows the right thing to do and fails to do it, for him it is sin" (v. 17). Should you keep your home on the sand?

These truths may be hitting you like a ton of bricks (pun intended). These truths might be stirring your soul in a way you've never felt before. These truths, regardless of how you feel about them, are truth.

Let's shift gears and talk about other causes and consequences.

Is it possible to trade future blessings for temporary pleasure? Yup. Read about causes and consequences in the story of Esau in Genesis 25:29-33.

If we seek the empty and fleeting promises and pleasures of the world, it will leave us empty and hungry over and over again. We may very well give up a blessing that God had in store for us and wants to give us. So, let's hunger and thirst for what matters. Read John 6:35. Jesus is the bread of life. He promises that all who come to Him won't hunger or thirst (also John 4).

In the previous verses of John chapter six, Jesus calls out the people following after Him for their carnal stomachs (v. 26). Have you ever heard the phrase, "You are what you eat?" I know that when I eat gobs of sugar and fried food, I feel like a lethargic, bloated, miserable human (it's okay, you can laugh!). Now, think about it in the spiritual context. When we feast on the world, we tend to take on depression, heaviness of heart, and bitterness walks all over us. In turn, we produce fruits of the same.

Ask yourself this and *journal* about it: When I become hungry and empty, do I feed on the things of the world or God's Word? Do I have a spiritual hunger, or am I ruled by a stomach for worldly pleasures?

Identify some ways you currently satisfy your "hunger" and further conclude if they're healthy or are worldly "junk food." What is the evidence? In other words, what fruit do you produce based off what you're eating?

Once you've identified the fruits you're producing, let's think about where they come from; let's examine your tree's roots.

Section 2: The Reality

Roots & Resolve

WHAT HAPPENS WHEN I LISTEN TO THE WORLD INSTEAD OF CHRIST?

"Every conflict stems from a wrong view of God."
—Rev. Mike Wingfield

As mentioned in the "A is for Apple" chapter, "Genesis" can mean the "root:" where something begins. Everything starts off small (one word, one picture, one text, one act), then matures, producing our reality. Reflect on the process below:

Seed → Roots→ Tree→ Fruit

Now, consider this analogy and how it pairs to the tree process:

Life → Thoughts→ Heart→ Actions

Let's focus on the roots/thoughts in this segment. Roots take nutrients from around their environment to grow. Thoughts are the same way. If the environment around our minds is saturated with lude images, coarse talk, lawlessness, constant negativity, etc., the sprouts and branches of our tree will bend and twist in those directions (ultimately producing fruit of the same). The more we're in the environment, the more natural the crooked way becomes to our psyche.

For me, the thoughts of something or someone better (thoughts from the world and the enemy) produced roots of discontentment. Discontentment's offspring is bitterness. I resented what I had and begrudged my spouse.

Comparison always kills contentment. Before I knew it, bitterness became the pattern for my life. It became natural for me to apathetically disengage from the reality God had so graciously given me with my spouse. Do you find yourself there today?

I'm praying that you are reading this book because, all of a sudden, those "natural" bends of bitterness and curves or cravings suddenly became foreign to you, as they became to me. God graced me with mercy and showed me what I was doing with my life. And let me tell you, I was one misshapen tree. Friend, it's time to correct destructive ways and straighten stems.

Heed this warning in Deuteronomy 29:18-19,

> Beware lest there be among you a man or woman or clan or tribe whose heart is turning away today from the Lord our God to go and serve the gods of those nations. Beware lest there be among you a root bearing poisonous and bitter fruit, one who, when he hears the words of this sworn covenant, blesses himself in his heart, saying, 'I shall be safe, though I

walk in the stubbornness of my heart.' This will lead to the sweeping away of moist and dry alike.

This passage is so rich with good teaching that we can learn from today!

1. Idols steal our heart away from God. Period.
2. A root (thoughts) is what bears actions (fruit).
3. The fruit is poisonous, affecting everyone who partakes in it!

   a. Bitterness and destructive negativity are contagious. Ever heard of the idiom, "One bad apple spoils the whole barrel?" I never wanted to be poisonous to those around me. I knew I needed to change.

4. This doesn't target unbelievers. "Turning away" infers that their hearts were once toward God. The context refers to someone who hears God's covenant and turns away to sin (Galatians 5:13).
5. The result is "sweeping away." The Hebrew *caphah* means "destruction." For more Scripture on the result, I urge you to read the convicting passage in James 3:14-18.

Is it time for your roots to make a nutrient shift? Allow Jesus to be the nourisher and the root in your life. Jesus, after all, is called the "root of Jesse" (Romans 15:12). And ladies, if you're like me, I want to abide in Him. Colossians 2:6-7 says, "Therefore, as you received Christ Jesus the Lord, so walk in Him, rooted and built up in Him and established in the faith, just as you were taught, abounding in thanksgiving."

Christ explained how He is the true vine in John 15:1-8, and if you want extra encouragement, read those verses. We need to strive to be continually attached to the *true* vine—it provides the authentic nutrients that our soul craves! You can't bear righteous fruit without it. The result is strong branches, unwavering against the wind and storms.

If you're attached to a bitter root (or worse, if you own one), you won't get any good nutrients from there! Remember that if you continue to hold onto and nourish the dysfunctional comfort of a bitter root, you are an easy target for the enemy to win your heart and take over your actions.

Ask the Lord to prune you of it and expect it to be painful. I say this because when those familiar habits are snipped, relearning healthy ones requires us to first deal with our own shortcomings. *Journal* about what you think is taking you away from His healing, spiritual nutrients and how you can hand over the shears to God.

May you resolve with steadfastness to redirect where you're getting nourishment from by establishing a clear and sturdy channel between the branch and the True Vine.

In grade school, we learn that seeds not only need good nutrients to grow; they also need sunlight. What better place to find that source for our spiritual seeds than the Son

Himself who is the Light? Let's get growing.

Light & Life

WHAT HAPPENS WHEN I FOLLOW THE DARK INSTEAD OF THE LIGHT?

"All the darkness in the world cannot extinguish the light of a single candle." —St. Francis of Assisi

Darkness desires to encompass. Sin desires to reign. False freedom desires our fragile hearts. So, let's shed some light on things.

The fourth verse in the Word of God declares how God saw the light that He created; it was good. Then, He separated it from darkness—not to co-exist. Before the Fall even happened, God separated ("divided" in some translations) the light from the dark. There was no grey area. No compromise.

Before God created the light, there was only darkness. Can you imagine?

Do a search on the effects of no sunlight on humans. Even within a small amount of time, there are psychological effects, physiological effects, and loss of the sense of time.

When I was a child, my family went camping in tents. No lights. No cellphones. Flashlights were turned off. What did I feel at nighttime? Utter terror and fear. I couldn't sleep.

Those nights were some of the most frightening nights of my life. Only when dawn came did I breathe a sigh of relief.

Are you there now? Are you in the dark, plagued by fear—your mind and body compromised by the effects? Have you lost track of time and space? Are you just drifting? Are you waiting, holding your breath for that distinctive ray of first light?

1 John 1:5 says, "This is the message we have heard from Him and proclaim to you, that God is light, and in Him is no darkness at all." We crave that light, don't we? You know deep down in your soul that you weren't meant for the dark, because we instinctively can't survive in utter darkness!

Even dabbling in darkness has its effects. We can't walk in both light and darkness. Isaiah 5:20 gives us a stark warning, "Woe to those who call evil good and good evil, who put darkness for light and light for darkness, who put bitter for sweet and sweet for bitter!" If that doesn't speak for itself, I'm not sure what does.

John 3:16 is a beloved passage, but let me challenge you today to look at its context. John 3:19-21 says,

> And this is the judgment: the light has come into the world, and people loved the darkness rather than the light because their works were evil. For everyone who does wicked things hates the light and does not come to the light, lest his works should be exposed. But whoever does what is true comes to the light, so that it may be clearly seen that his works have been carried out in God.

If you're dabbling in darkness, as I was, this is your wake-up call. Read that passage one more time and take a moment to *journal* about how it resonates with you.

Now, read Ephesians 5:8 (I challenge you to read the eye-opening context, as well). We weren't always children of light. At one time, we were in darkness (Ephesians 2:1-10). But then, one glorious day, we accepted Christ as Lord and Savior, and now we are in the light of the Lord. As children of Light, we need to be separate from the advice and teachings of the wicked (Psalm 1:1). We are commanded to walk (an action word, which also means "to live") as children of Light, because in doing so, we glorify the One who gave us that light.

When we believed upon the Lord, we obtained something more powerful than darkness. Our light doesn't come from ourselves—it comes from God. If we are to wield the light, all glory goes to the One who gave us that light. Psalm 27:1 says, "The Lord is my light and my salvation; whom shall I fear? The Lord is the stronghold of my life; of whom shall I be afraid?"

Fear can't stand against God's light. Darkness can't stand against it. We can be confident in His Light, because it *will* overcome darkness (Scripture Sprint: John 1:5; Revelation 21:23-25; 22:5).

Forget the yin and the yang. Forget the balance of a "force." Light *will* rule. Do not be fooled. Cling to the Light, and in doing so, you choose life.

Let's go one step further with Matthew 5:14-16 to

understand what light has to do with our role in Christ:

> You (*that's us!*) are the light of the world. A city set on a hill cannot be hidden. Nor do people light a lamp and put it under a basket, but on a stand, and it gives light to all in the house. In the same way, let your light shine before others, so that they may see your good works and give glory to your Father who is in heaven (emphasis added).

We are a living, breathing light in the world—reflections of the true Light for all to see. That's why it's so important to live as children of Light. John 8:12 says, "Again Jesus spoke to them, saying, 'I am the light of the world. Whoever follows Me *will not walk in darkness*, but will have the light of life'" (emphasis added).

Sister, it's time to *take hold* of the Light that lives within you to eradicate the darkness. *Take hold* of these truths and don't let your light be put under a basket.

You were released from darkness and chains the moment you surrendered to God's will. It didn't mean, however, that darkness would give up trying to snatch you. It meant that you have God on your side with His light to battle it.

If you're struggling with these truths, or if you openly revolt against the evidence of a new life, are you truly in the light and following Jesus? Ask yourself these questions:

1. Do I obey Him? 1 John 2:3-6. *Be careful that your obedience stems from gratitude and not obligation.*
2. Do I truly love the Lord and love whom He calls me to love? 1 John 2:7-11. *Note those amazing passages on light and dark!*
3. Is there evidence of growth, or is my growth atrophied due to a disconnect between me and the light source? See Hebrews 5:14.

If you aren't connected to the light source, which is Jesus Christ, not much more of this book will make sense. However, I am confident that the Word of God can warm hearts of any climate, so let's keep going.

Heed the words from Ecclesiastes 2:13-14, "Then I saw that there is more gain in wisdom than in folly, as there is more gain in light than in darkness. The wise person has his eyes in his head, but the fool walks in darkness."

1 John 1:7 says, "But *if* we walk in the light, as He is in the light, we have fellowship with one another, and the blood of Jesus his Son cleanses us from all sin" (emphasis added).

I emphasized "if" because that denotes a choice. You have a choice today, sister. I pray that you choose to abandon any and all ways of darkness and purpose to follow the Light and claim the power of the Light as a child of light.

What happens when we do this? Let's restate the above verse: when we walk in that light, fellowship with others (especially our husbands) is restored and we are forgiven of our sins—what a beautiful result!

Journal about your new discoveries and determinations regarding light and dark.

We need to be fully awake to the light. We need to embrace it. We'd be blind without it. Can anyone fight in the dark? They'd be . . . well . . . open and vulnerable to enemy attack, to say the least. No soldier wants to find themselves in that place! If you have your sword handy and the Light to guide your way, let's venture on. The following two chapters will unmask our true enemy and shed light upon the ruses meant to ensnare us. Are you ready?

Section 3: The Ruse

Intro

This segment of *The Apple* should not be overlooked. I realize, sister, that you have a deep desire to be freed and may want to skip over these chapters to the "how to" ones. However, the words within "The Ruse" are paramount. Exposing the enemy for who he is and understanding his tactics and how he knows you, plays a vital part in understanding how to battle current and future attacks . . . and not just regarding EAs.

In "The Ruse," we'll go over the importance of unmasking the real enemies of your soul, humbly realize what the Bible says about the enemies' ruses, and begin to formulate a battle plan. Onward, Warrior Wives and Warrior Women.

Foe & Folly

WHO IS THE TRUE FOE?

"We can't choose when or where we meet the enemy."
—Rev. Jeff Dunkle

Okay, sisters, so we find ourselves here. Know that this

book cannot possibly encompass all we should know about the enemy and his tactics. I strived to zero in on the specific tactics he uses in an EA, offering the greatest relevance. Let's move forward undaunted.

This chapter is not a Sunday school lesson. I won't depict our enemy as painted red with horns. You may be surprised to know that our enemy, called Satan, (I do not like to hear, see, or speak his name, so this will be the only time you will see it in this book) is a "glorious being" of God's creation—many scholars agree that he was a high-ranking angel (Isaiah 14:12-15, KJV; Revelation 12:7-12; and I also like Jude 8-9). I do not want to cultivate the unhealthy study of demons by any means. If you want greater insight with unmatched relevance, read C. S. Lewis' *Screwtape Letters*. I simply want to explain what we are up against.

Throughout the past years, months, or weeks that you may have been involved in an EA, what or who do you define as your "enemy?"

Be vulnerable, as I'm about to: I considered my husband my enemy . . . then myself . . . then the EA . . . then everyone. It was at that moment in my thinking that the Lord revealed to me who the true foe was: the enemy was working through the hearts and minds of my husband, me, and the EA in order to cause distrust. I shut everyone out. There is no denying who our true foe is, sister. Read Ephesians 6:12.

In my WIP fiction novel, *Pure Heart*, I have a chapter named "The True Foe," because sometimes, ladies, we get confused about who the true foe is. He loves using the blame game. And he wants us to be so confused that we place blame on others, our circumstances, our habits, our upbringing, etc., causing us to minimalize the destructiveness of our choices.

He is the master of deception and confusion (see 2 Corinthians 11:14 just for a start!). And he's been at it for a *long* time. So, please . . . there is no need to feel like a failure if you didn't initially see the wolf in the sheep's clothing.

Speaking of which, no one has to guess what happens when a wolf gets inside a sheep pen. Even still, sometimes we have a misguided compassion and turn a blind eye to the reality that the odd-looking sheep we allowed into our pen is, in actuality, a wolf.

Interestingly, in my little ESV concordance, the word "wolf" is between "wife" and "woman," dividing the two words. Now, read John 10:12. The wolf scatters the sheep. In the Greek, the word for "scatter" is painted this way: "to fly in all directions—usually not in the direction we need to go." The result? Isolation, fear, division, danger, injury, or even death.

If you think that's being a little harsh on the wolf's intentions, consider this: The enemy isn't going to come to you in plain sight with a large warning sign dipped in blood. He's going to come to you in beauty carrying a banner of false peace, false freedom, and everything you think you need (read 2 Peter 2 in its entirety and brace yourself).

The enemy won't tantalize us with beautiful truth—

only beautiful lies. The enemy twists, muddies, shades, and camouflages the truth.

I'll give you examples from my own life . . .

1. Lie – that I could be free in my EA. I took care of my home, had small children, was overworked with two jobs, had few friends, and had a workaholic husband. I felt stuck. The EA was a fantasy—a getaway from the normal routine and duties, which is why the lie was so enticing to me. I found that sin never leads to freedom—maybe refining, testing, punishment, but never freedom.

2. Lie – that I was truly loved in my EA. Ha . . . girl, did I fall deep into this one! Only after the Lord redeemed me did I put the puzzle pieces together. I discovered that the love for my husband was the *true* love intended to display Jesus' perfect plan and that the enemy had sinister plans for lust—not love.

The enemy wants to get you comfortable enough with his lies in order to make you vulnerable. But ladies, there is no true comfort in a lie. I initially found comfort, but when the deception was revealed, there was absolutely no comfort to be found.

Let me say it again. The enemy wants to get you comfortable enough with his lies in order to make you vulnerable. Vulnerability leads to compromise. This is something I am sure I do not have to explain, because we are keenly aware that more and more compromise leads to enslavement of mind, heart, body, and spirit—and that's exactly what the enemy of our souls wants.

After eating a fortune cookie once, I took a second glance at what I read inside: "Compromise is always wrong if it means sacrificing a principle." If the world can make such a statement about breaking morals, we, as Christians, need to be more sensitive to the severity of the consequences of compromise when it affects our faith and steadfast belief in God's Word.

Psalm 40:4, "Blessed is the man who makes the Lord his trust, who does not turn to the proud, to those who go astray after a lie." How quick we are to point out when someone else is following a lie, but when we are hearing those beautiful lies we want to hear, how quickly we go astray after them as sheep!

The cure? According to that verse, keeping our path out of the way of pride and lies is a result of making the Lord our trust. This is similar to trusting in God, but this verse goes much deeper, so we should, too. In Greek, *mibtach*, trust can mean, "confiding in, the object of our confidence, or security." Wow. In your EA, did/do you seek those things? Someone to confide in? Someone who superficially gave you confidence? Someone you felt secure with?

Ladies, did we replace making the Lord our trust with making the EA our trust? Think about that for a long minute and *journal* about it.

Thankfully, for the child of God, the Spirit doesn't hesitate to stir within us when a lie is creeping in. To be honest, I pushed aside the Spirit's warnings and suffered because I didn't listen.

I urge you to heed the subtle promptings of the Spirit. For me, it was just as clear as a warning sign—a stomach twisting, anxiety-type heart palpitation that disguised itself as excitement. It's the best way I can describe it. But for me, it was the Spirit's way of throwing up a red flag. Now I call it a "Spirit Stir."

If you experience one of these or your own unmistakable "Spirit Stir," listen to it (ask the Lord to show you through His Word). Be open to it (be willing to accept what He shows you). Be in tune with it (once accepted, follow it).

If you're still not convinced that you are being lied to by the enemy through your EA, have you considered that you are lying to yourself?

Before you recoil at that, know that *any* Christian can fall prey to "logically" denying sin—trying to minimalize the damage it could cause. I'm a logical person. But even I tried to reason with myself that the EA was permissible. I wanted to justify my actions because of my feelings.

Anyone can influence themselves to believe false logic through feelings and, therefore, deny reality. Take the "post-truth" phenomenon permeating our culture, for instance. By Google definition, post-truth is, "relating to or denoting circumstances in which objective facts are less influential in shaping public opinion than appeals to emotion and personal belief." In other words, people are led by and believe feelings instead of facts.

Thinking that it is permissible to love an EA is post-truth mentality. That's a bold statement, isn't it? Not when you recall that as a Christian, we cannot have truth without love or love without truth. We, as Christians, need to challenge our "truth" to the truth of God's Word—no matter how painful that may be.

Furthermore, to combat logic, you need to use logic. I was using feelings. Today, if you're finding yourself in that gray area of coming up with reasons why your EA is "justified" based off your feelings, I challenge you to compare your logic with the logic of the Word of God. You'll find that what God has already said is enough.

Feelings are inherent, yes, but they have great potential to be motivated by our sin nature. If you're struggling with post-truth mentality, answer these questions with fact (not feeling): Am I being loving to my husband when I exhibit sacred marital love toward someone else? Am I following God's Word and His guidelines for marriage and holy love? Am I being selfish in my words, thoughts, and actions? Am I trying to disguise lies with "logic?" Am I using God's grace as a license to do what I want to do? (Scripture Sprint: Romans 6:1-2,15; Galatians 5:13; Jude 4 in the NIV). Breathe . . . I know this may be difficult. Pray . . . and *journal* about your answers.

The wool needs to be taken off our eyes. We need to be on high alert.

1 Peter 5:8, "Be sober-minded; be watchful. Your adversary the devil prowls around like a roaring lion, seeking someone to devour."

So therefore . . . Matthew 26:41, "Watch and pray that you may not enter into temptation. The spirit indeed is willing, but the flesh is weak."

The Greek for "watch" is *gregoreo*, and it means to continuously be watching, paying strict attention. When we aren't on high alert, enemy attacks intensify in-step with our increasing apathy and compromise. In other words, when we become dull and desensitized to the truth, we allow spiritual attacks to increase.

It's time to wake up and remember who our enemy is and what he intends for us!

When we chose to follow Christ, we became instant targets and enemies of the world (John 15:18-19; James 4:4 says this in the inverse). The world and the enemy's intention for us is not life. It is death.

But do not fear! The attacks can't take us from life in our Heavenly Father. Strike up your courage with Joshua 1:9 and 1 Corinthians 16:13.

While we are still on this earth, we will be daily confronted with the lies of the enemy since we are friends of God. The scriptural examples of the enemy's lies were too numerous to include—I was floored! The enemy has a time-tested battle plan against us and a snapshot of it is below:

1. Clouds the mind

    Result: confusion in prayer, purpose, relationships, and path

2. Distractions/Busyness

    Result: gives us a convenient excuse to ignore our spouse and healthy support systems

3. Thoughts of failure

    Result: defeatist attitude, "Why even try to make my marriage work?"

4. Temps us with something or someone "better"

    Result: dilutes reality, creates a pining for fantasy.

5. Whispers the world's knowledge and advice vs. God's wisdom and the Word

    Result: even more confusion/poor decisions if we're not rooted in God's Word.

6. Dissention

    Result: self-righteous anger, resulting in isolation of spouse, friends, and family.

7. Breaks down our self-image and self-worth

    Result: temps us to allow pain/suffering willingly because we think we deserve it or because we feel that we aren't "good enough." We forget God's deep love for us, His beloved.

8. Weakens us with lies to the point of being apathetic

    Result: callousness creates a spirit of unwillingness to change, heal, forgive, or simply care. Apathy opens us up completely to enemy attack.

Now, feel free to write in this book and put a checkmark next to each way the enemy has attacked you. You know the enemy has a plan to defeat you. Do you have a battle plan to fend off the enemy? Just as Jesus battled and won against the tempting of the enemy in the book of Matthew, know that Scripture is the number one way to combat our common enemy. I'm sure all followers of Jesus know this. So, let's take this a step further.

Like football players who study how their opponent played in previous games, think about how the enemy has "played" in your past. Get your *journal* ready to answer these questions: How did the enemy work in your past? What did he whisper to you? What moves did he make? Do you see any patterns of his tactics? Now, write about how you could have better combatted the enemy.

Chances are, that when you were writing about his tactics, you wrote down people he may have used to charm or deceive you. It's no secret that the enemy of our souls uses others to carry out his work. And it can be through other people. The next chapter talks about this. They are called "false prophets" in the Bible. You may be thinking to yourself: *but those are a thing of the past!* Think again. Why would the Bible have so many instances and Scripture warning against them if they were just in that era, in that country, during that time? Because those who operate under malevolent sway are still alive and well today.

Not convinced? Recall our conversations about the wolf and the sheep. Remember the intentions of the wolf, lies of the wolf, and the result of letting the wolf in. Now, take a breath. It's time to unmask the wolves for what they really are.

Matthew 7:15, "Beware of *false prophets,* who come to you in sheep's clothing but inwardly are *ravenous wolves*" (emphasis added). Let's journey on.

Foe & Folly

WHO ARE THE FALSE PROPHETS IN MY LIFE?

"The forces of evil did not disappear when Jesus left the earth." —Kenneth Boa[4]

Metaphors are a wonderful way to explain spiritual truths in simple terms. The verse in Matthew likened false prophets to wolves. In the chapter of *The Apple* you just read, John 10 is mentioned, where Jesus describes Himself as the Shepherd and His followers as the sheep. Read the entirety of John chapter 16, then return here (*journal* if you feel led).

My husband always told me that he was my protector—my "sheepdog." God gave my husband to me as a sheepdog to keep me (a sheep) safe. There are so many wolves in disguise trying to sway our hearts and affection. As sheep, we need to first be aware of the Good Shepherd and our relationship with Him. Second, we need to respect the sheepdog God placed over us (just like the husband/wife metaphor with Christ being over the church, Ephesians 5:22-33). Third, in heeding the words of both, we, ourselves, need to be vigilant for wolves.

The sheepdog doesn't have the same authority the Good Shepherd does, but rather, the sheepdog's master is *my* master, too! The sheepdog has a responsibility to obey the Shepherd's commands. When I think of my husband being what he is intended to be, it calms me.

If your sheepdog is "sleeping on the job," isn't a Christ follower, or is blatantly disobeying the commands of the Good Shepherd, please seek professional Christian counseling and be in consistent prayer for your sheepdog.

The Google definition of "deceivers" is: "to mislead by a false appearance or statement; delude." Read Matthew 13:24-30, which you may recognize as the parable of the wheat and the tares. Tares do not have obvious differences from true wheat. By appearances, they look like us and can talk like us, but consider the words of John MacArthur, Jr. in his book, *The Gospel According to Jesus*: "The sons of the Evil One can imitate the children of the kingdom, but they cannot produce true righteousness."[5]

Furthermore, 2 Corinthians 11:13-15 describes them this

way, "For such men are false apostles, deceitful workmen, disguising themselves as apostles of Christ. And no wonder, for even Satan disguises himself as an angel of light. So it is no surprise if his servants, also, disguise themselves as *servants of righteousness*. Their end will correspond to their deeds" (emphasis added).

False prophets may be good at disguises, but their deeds will expose them for who they really are. You can sniff them out by their fruits (Matthew 7:15-20). Consider the individual you may be involved in an EA with: What's their life like and what choices have they made? How do they interact with others? Are they married? If so, how are they treating their spouse? One way to find out is how they disrespect their spouse by initiating/continuing relationship with you. Painful to hear, but true.

For specific examples of godless fruit, read 2 Timothy 3:1-7. Take special notice of verses six and seven, which focus on their intentions for women of the home (us).

If you believe that they are true wheat, what evidence is there?

Speaking of wheat, let's talk about bread. Galatians 5:9 says, "A little leaven leavens the whole lump." Now read 1 Corinthians 5:6-7. See any similarities?

Consequently, 1 Corinthians 15:33 says, "Do not be deceived: 'Bad company ruins good morals.'" This quote is from an extra-canonical text from Menander's comedy, "Thais." Study the word for "company" (*homilia* in the Greek). It's quite interestingly defined as, "companionship, intercourse, communion." That's strong language, which makes for a stark warning!

This type of company includes intellectual, emotional, and spiritual intimacy through sharing ideas, thoughts, and feelings. Being vulnerable here . . . I fell into that trap. If I really reflect upon it, I fed upon the intimate ideas, thoughts, and feelings on an intellectual and spiritual level. I walked right into the wolf's alluring trap, which was set with delectable words, tantalizing my mind and emotions.

Ephesians 5:6-7, "Let no one deceive you with empty words, for because of these things the wrath of God comes upon the sons of disobedience. Therefore, do not become partners with them." Have you been deceived by empty words as I was? At the time, I considered the words he spoke to be inspired and eloquent. In the end, they proved empty.

We are warned not to become partners/partakers with people who speak such things. Their words may be beautiful on the outside and sweet to the taste but void of truth and any good thing.

Colossians 2:8, "See to it that no one takes you captive by philosophy and empty deceit, according to human tradition, according to the elemental spirits of the world, and not according to Christ." This verse hit me hard, because I felt I had a deep, even spiritual, "connection" with the EA.

If you are convinced, as I was, that you have a "connection" with an EA and obsess over it, consider the definition of "obsess": "An idea or thought that continually preoccupies or intrudes a person's mind."[6] If you openly admit you have an obsession, or even if you're denying an obsession, read the definition one more time and focus on the word, "intrudes."

Let's go one step further: who or what has preoccupied your mind so much that it has become an intruder? You wouldn't let an intruder into your home, your church, or your place of work. Why would you swing the door wide to invite an intruder into your mind? Whatever that intruder is, selfishness, loneliness, hate, bitterness and/or the EA you're involved in, be aware that deep turbulence will be experienced.

2 John is a letter to "the chosen lady and her children." It is a letter written to her in order to encourage her to walk in the truth. 2 John 7-11 is of great consequence to our focus here. It says,

> For *many* deceivers have gone out into the world, those who do not confess the coming of Jesus Christ in the flesh. Such a one is the deceiver and the antichrist. Watch yourselves, so that you may not lose what we have worked for, but may win a full reward. Everyone who goes on ahead and does not *abide* in the teaching of Christ, does not have God. Whoever abides in the teaching has both the Father and the Son. If anyone comes to you and does not bring this teaching, *do not receive him into your house or give him any greeting*, for whoever greets him *takes part*

in his wicked works (emphases added).

This passage speaks specifically of the acceptance of the second coming of Christ. However, one can easily draw the conclusion that a godless person with lawless fruits is in a similar category as these deceivers. If someone is not for Christ, they are against Him.

Read those verses one more time. What have you worked for in your home and family? Have you received the EA into your house or even into the home of your mind and heart? Do you support and enflame deceit by building resentment toward your spouse and marriage?

Journal about your thoughts on this passage, which was possibly written to a woman and her children or "the church." Either way, that's us! It may as well have been written as a loving warning for you and for me.

Beloved, take the time right now and read these crucial passages: 1 John 2:18-27; 3:7-10; 4:1-6. We are warned time and time again, aren't we?

All of these truths and realities may be tough to stomach, and I realize this. Especially since the time spent with your EA has revolved around building walls brick-by-brick. You may have built a complete foundation or even an entire way of life from building those walls.

Deception compounds over time, but shedding light on it eradicates it immediately. I want this for your life: for you to see how precious and loved you are as a child of God, bought by His Son's blood. That is why I am urging you to test these wolves, these false prophets. As 1 Thessalonians 5:21 says, "Test everything. Hold onto the good." The good is the Word of God. Hold onto it, so you can avoid every kind of evil (v. 22).

Sniffing out the wolves is commendable, however, don't forget one critical step to recovery: **remember your first love—Christ**.

The church of Ephesus, in Revelation 2:1-7, properly weeded out the false prophets, but God still held against them the fact that they forgot their first love. Do not let this be true of you. Their first love was God, and when we acknowledge Him as our first love, His commands and His design for marriage will be honored.

God loves us with a fierce love, and He has a rightful and righteous jealousy for His Bride. "Be careful Christians (you that are married to Christ); remember, you are married to a jealous Husband!"—Charles H. Spurgeon. See Isaiah 54:5.

Before we delve into the next segment that takes us on the route to redemption and remembering our true first love, let's wrap up these chapters by thinking about these two things:

1. Do I know the Word of God well enough to have the ability to detect moral or doctrinal error? 2 Timothy 2:15. To quote my own father, "Knowing God's truth and living by it will protect me from spiritual deception." You are protected if you know it, live it,

and recall that it won't return empty (Isaiah 55:10-11). Otherwise, you are an easy target for spiritual deception.

2. Am I making excuses for the wolf in my sheep pen? Not everyone who claims they're from God truly is. It can be as simple as making you guess the Word of God—that their own words are above it. See also Galatians 1:9 for the result.

Be encouraged by Psalm 27:11-14,

Teach me your way, O Lord, and lead me on a level path because of my enemies. Give me not up to the will of my adversaries; for false witnesses have risen against me, and they breathe out violence. I believe that I shall look upon the goodness of the Lord in the land of the living! Wait for the Lord; be strong, and let your heart take courage; wait for the Lord!

The next chapter will take us through the main deception of the enemy through EAs. Just as the enemy disguises himself as an angel of light, he's quite good at disguising lust as love.

Love & Lust

WHY DOES THE MIND MATTER?

"There is a God-shaped vacuum in the heart of each man, which cannot be satisfied by any created thing but only

by God the Creator, made known through Jesus Christ."
—Blaise Pascal

Before we delve into this soul-searching chapter, you must know one very important thing: God does not tempt us with lust. We may be tested through trials that involve lust, but God never tempts us. James 1:13-15 says, "Let no one say when he is tempted, 'I am being tempted by God,' for God cannot be tempted with evil, and He Himself tempts no one. But each person is tempted when he is lured and enticed by his own desire. Then desire when it has conceived gives birth to sin, and sin when it is fully grown brings forth death."

Take heart! If the powerful grip of mental, emotional, and/or physical lust has a hold on you today, let the words of 1 Corinthians 10:13 comfort you, "No temptation has overtaken you that is not common to man. God is faithful, and He will not let you be tempted beyond your ability, but with the temptation he will also provide the way of escape, that you may be able to endure it." Aren't you so very thankful for a God that does not tempt us and also provides a way of escape (if we are humble enough to take it)? Our faithful and living God knows our mortal struggles and provides a way for us.

He not only knows our struggle, Jesus (fully God and fully man) actively battled it, too. The Lord's Prayer (Jesus' example of how to pray) includes, "And lead us not into temptation, but deliver us from evil." He is praying for God to not lead us into temptation. It's important to note that God leading us into temptation doesn't lead to sin but to testing. Hard to think about? Go ahead and read Matthew 4:1-11. If Jesus, the Son of God, wasn't exempt from testing, we aren't either.

Read Hebrews 4:15; 2:18. Jesus knows very well what we go through daily. We are not alone on our journey, and if we hold the hand of the One who has already walked the path of temptation through trials, we can feel secure in knowing that He is trustworthy and true. If we let go of His hand and allow that temptation to become sin . . . well, that's up to us. God knows what trials can produce in us. They are a way that God shows His love. "Tough love," if you will. He wants us to trust Him and have faith in Him, and what better way than being in situations where we must rely on Him for victory. Through trials, we have the opportunity for growth and a new, heavenward mindset.

Romans 12:2 says, "Do not be conformed to this world, but be transformed by the renewal of your mind, that by testing you may discern what is the will of God, what is good and acceptable and perfect." Did you notice the same thing I did in this verse? Testing is also a way for us to know what the will of God is (also see Deuteronomy 13:1-5; James 1:1-3). Whether you believe it or not, you're being tested through your EA, who is begging you (directly or indirectly) to conform to the world. The ways of the world. The selfishness of the world. The trends. The feelings. The sensuality. The lies. Sister, don't give in any longer.

Anyone is susceptible to the alluring temptation of lust—no one is exempt. The word "lust" is found 77x in the King James Version of the Bible. In later versions, "lust" is replaced by passions, desires, and wanton cravings. No matter how the English language puts it, "burning with lust/ inflamed" (Romans 1:27) in the Greek means a literal blaze. They are strong feelings that when provoked, intensify. Lust is a sin that can engulf us as it travels from our eyes, to our minds, to our hearts, to our actions—much like Eve's fall.

The result, much like an actual fire, is destruction. As it says later in James 4, those desires produce quarrels and fights. We see the first "blame game" with Adam and Eve (Genesis 2:11-13)! Have you experienced any of these lately in your marriage? I experienced them weekly, if not daily. It was only later when I realized how my selfish wants and discontentment played a huge role in the rift that was my marriage.

Over time, I had convinced myself that my marriage was not true love due to those frequent quarrels. When, in actuality, lust for the EA was disguised as love . . . and I was overtaken by it, producing dissension.

Recall the "wolf in sheep's clothing" metaphor and consider how lust similarly disguises itself as love. Lust is a vicious beast in the form of a person, image, or thought that crouches at the door of our affections and psyche. And it can strike at any moment—spontaneously even (stark contrast to love, which is a commitment of time and intentional effort).

Look at 2 Samuel 11:2 to see how quickly lust can capture us: "It happened, late one afternoon, when David arose from his couch and was walking on the roof of the king's house, that he saw from the roof a woman bathing; and the woman was very beautiful." You're encouraged to read the rest of this passage if you are unfamiliar with the outcome. Let me just say, a quote from the Daily Walk Bible encapsulates the result well: "We lose the peace of years when we hunt after the rapture of moments."[7]

Notice in the 2 Samuel passage above that the words, "it happened" came first—before the explanation! That is often how lust (which is a sinful connection) can happen. Instantly. David was simply arousing from a nap and "it happened!" One innocent action can lead to temptation; that's why we must stay on our guard. Constantly. As Charles H. Spurgeon said, "As you are tempted without ceasing, so pray without ceasing." More on this in a later chapter.

You may be thinking to yourself, *Self, it wasn't lust-at-first-sight, so maybe the EA really is love?* I thought the same thing. Many times. However, after being on my knees in prayer countless moments, I came to realize that the spark of emotional connection was the first step in the process that led to full-out lust.

Lust is a sneaky counterfeit of love. It took time to develop those feelings/thoughts into lustful reactions, mimicking the bond that love creates.

Whether the EA for you was an instant attraction, or one built over time, it equates to lust if it is not your rightful husband. Scripture supports this in Matthew 5:28, when Jesus confirmed that the initial thought ultimately leads to the action.

Those words may be sudden and jarring to you, so please, take time and *journal* your thoughts. If you're still struggling with lust vs. love, take a breath and recap what we know the Word of God says.

We know that real love is to know God (1 John 4:7-8). When we see that God embodies true love, He sacrificed for us, wants to spend time with us and call upon Him/rely on Him, and wants us to praise Him through our gifts, our view on love is perfected.

We know that there is no fear in true love. Being in a state of fear of punishment means we missed the mark on love in its pure sense (1 John 4:15-18).

We know that our desires put us at enmity with God and the Spirit and that we need to humble ourselves (James 4:1-10; Romans 8:5-14).

We know that the moral standard can be found in Jesus. He set the standard. He is the standard (Matthew 5:48 - found only a few verses away from Jesus' talk on lust).

We know that love isn't just about following the rules. Josh McDowell said that "rules without relationships equals rebellion"[8] and wow how true that is! If we just try to follow the rules/law/commandments without knowing and loving the God who spoke them, there is greater room for rebellion in our lives.

We know that when there is a substitute for Christ, it's called an "idol." Largely in Scripture, idols are depicted as solid forms, tangible. Therefore, in our culture, we largely tend to think nothing of it. However, today, we experience idols much like the ones described in Habakkuk 1:11 and Colossians 3:5. Consider how we tend to treat non-tangible idols the same way tangible ones are treated. We put our hopes in it . . . our dreams . . . our future and security. We set our hearts on it. Sometimes, we even praise or worship it by giving it our full admiration and time.

Gee, do I wish I could just swing a tangible axe at a tangible idol instead of dealing with that old nature! Destroying "unseen" idols is a constant internal battle of the mind and heart.

There is a remedy! 1 Corinthians 10:14 (just one verse after the temptation verse) says, "Therefore, flee from idolatry." The object of your temptation can be an idol. Is it a person? A feeling? Lustful thoughts? Flee.

If you're sensing that you're out of control or think that you can't combat this on your own, read Ezekiel 36:25-26. By God's good grace and mercy, He can give you a new heart. Are you humble enough to accept it? *Journal* your thoughts.

By this point, we are fully aware that inward, lustful

thoughts lead to outward lustful responses. Whether it's in picture form, descriptive words, and/or even actions, the next section will tackle the reality of those connections in our lives and marriage.

Love & Lust

WHY IS MY TEMPLE IMPORTANT?

"The best way of casting out an impure affection is to admit a pure one; and by the love of what is good, to expel the love of what is evil." —Thomas Chalmers, D.D., LL.D.[9]

The Word of God says that our bodies are sacred temples, not to be tarnished or put on display for others to lust after. This needs special attention, ladies, so let's get a cup of coffee or tea and dive in.

Newsflash: we don't need anyone worshipping the temple of our bodies or giving it praise. This goes against what's socially circulated and acceptable. In our self/success/sex-focused society, we're bombarded with messages that shout, "Make him desire you . . . indulge yourself . . . you deserve happiness regardless of the cost . . . be the skinniest/sexiest/best version of yourself . . . love is whatever you want it to be . . . you can have it all."

It's an uphill battle wrestling the world and our human

nature, isn't it? The innate desire for our bodies to be looked upon with favor is fueled by the feeling of gratification upon someone's praise. When that "someone" is not our husband, we are in the realm of immediate danger (more about this in the next chapter).

Read Ephesians 4:17-24 for a reality check. After reading those truths, the words from the world and our human nature seem sick, don't they?

Even so, it's no wonder that when we are daily pressed and pressured from society, media, social media, and friends (and even ourselves!) that we fall so easily into the trap of accepting lustful and deceptive words. It's what we wanted to hear! Or so we thought . . . Now read 1 John 2:15-17. The once-beautiful words will fall short. The ego boost won't last. Our bodies will decay. The desire will fizzle out. All that matters in the end is the Lord, His Word, and His will.

When I realized this, it dawned on me . . . I wasn't meant to be someone's addiction or obsession. I wasn't meant to be someone's faith or "savior." I wasn't meant to be someone's fun or fantasy. Ladies, we don't exist to fulfill anyone's sexual desires, ego, status, or anything else. We don't exist to fill boredom or a void in human hearts. We don't exist to embody a role that we were biblically never meant to fill. Oftentimes, Proverbs calls married women "forbidden" women. We are claimed. Unavailable. Not to be touched by another man.

It's time to take care of our ailing temple.

As Christ followers, we know the temple is a sacred place that God created—not a souvenir shop. What you do with your body is important, because it is not your own. Read Matthew 21:12-13, then 1 Corinthians 6:19-20, and *journal* about how you think God reacts to anyone defiling, or being allowed to defile your body's temple in word, thought, or deed.

Don't let the enemy rule any inch of your temple, defiling the sacredness that God placed inside. Sinful desires will wage war against our temples, barraging each stone, pillar, and room until we reach Glory (1 Peter 2:11-12). Sister, I am yelling, "we need to be prepared for battle" from the rooftops!

So, let's prepare for battle from those temple rooftops.

How? Train your heart to feel what your mind knows. Read that once more. You know truth, Christian. It's time to hold fast to it and train your heart.

How is that possible? Isn't the heart wicked? Yes, God did say the heart is "desperately wicked/deceitful" and questioned who could know it (Jeremiah 17:9).

However, that doesn't mean we don't try to guard our hearts (Philippians 4:7). Proverbs 4:23 says, "Keep your heart with all vigilance, for from it flow the springs of life." The Hebrew word *mishmar* for diligence/vigilance is the same word used for a guard that kept watch over a prisoner in a cell. That's a significant job!

Once you . . .

1. Recognize earthly pain vs. eternal pain in light of consequences
2. Believe divine truth over sugar-coated lies
3. Remember heaven in perspective over the temporal
4. Feast on God's Word instead of fleshly indulgences

. . . your mind is ready to train your heart. You can persevere, my friends (James 1:12)! Let's take this Psalm from King David and God's Word to help us:

Psalm 101:2-4, "I will ponder the way that is blameless. Oh when will You come to me? I will walk with integrity of heart within my house; I will not set before my eyes anything that is worthless. I hate the work of those who fall away; it shall not cling to me. A perverse heart shall be far from me; I will know nothing of evil."

Let's break that down into something deeper that we can grasp today (also Proverbs 4:23-27):

1. Talk with God about your walk. Express your intentionality to Him.
2. Purpose to seek the Lord and wait with expectation.
3. Aim to display the heart you'd want your loved ones to emulate.
4. Guard your eyes. Have you ever heard that popular quote (attributed to Shakespeare, DaVinci, or Cicero) that "the eyes are the window to the soul?" What we take in through our eyes is translated by our minds

(read Matthew 6:22-23). If we continuously view evil/destruction/lust/hate, our minds will be filled with thoughts of such, making little room for the light to come in. Contrastingly, if we fix our eyes (Psalm 119:6, 15; Hebrews 12:2, NIV) on light and the goodness of God, we make room for even more light to pour in! Open up the shutters of the windows of your eyes. Let the sunlight of God's true love in!

5. Know what to hate. (Scripture Sprint: Psalm 11:5; 45:7; 97:10; 119:113; 163; Isaiah 61:8; Amos 5:15; Romans 12:9). We are not to hate people; we are to hate evil (1 John 4:20; Matthew 5:43-48). Recognize you aren't hating a person. You're hating the result of sin in your life and sin itself.

6. Don't let it "cling" to you. The Hebrew word is *dabaq*, which is a verb/action word: "to stay with, keep close, to be joined together, or pursue closely, or to allow to overtake." Has your EA "clung" to you in any of these ways? Be honest with yourself and *journal* about it.

7. The last phrase is proclaiming that our hearts, in turn, will depart or be removed, and that, in doing so, (hence the semi-colon used in the verse) we won't know wickedness. How freeing!

We aren't to be slaves to the flesh any longer (Galatians 5:24). 1 Peter 4:1-6 says we need to, " . . . live for the rest of the time in the flesh no longer for human passions but for the will of God."

My prayer for all of God's beloved daughters, "Father, cure us of the lust of the flesh and teach us something truly satisfying." Psalm 90:14, "Satisfy us in the morning with Your steadfast love, that we may rejoice and be glad all our days."

Let's close this chapter with some encouraging words that catapult us toward the truth.

> Titus 2:11-14,
> For the grace of God has appeared, bringing salvation for all people, training us to renounce ungodliness and worldly passions, and to live self-controlled, upright, and godly lives in the present age, waiting for our blessed hope, the appearing of the glory of our great God and Savior Jesus Christ, who gave Himself for us to redeem us from all lawlessness and to purify for Himself a people for his own possession who are zealous for good works.

In the end, God will not ask us if we followed our heart but if we kept it pure.

Section 4: The Route

Intro

Here we are, ladies. As it says in John 14:4-6, Jesus *is* the way: the literal path. In Acts, they called the early church followers of "the Way." We are *still* people of the one true way. If we know Jesus, we know the way.

"The Route" is where we take wing, using God-given spiritual weaponry to combat the world, our enemy, and our sinful nature that wages war. Let's gain the momentum of confidence in Christ to launch us forward. Let's start swinging with what will beat down the dark and make a path to freedom!

Vows & Verdicts

HOW SHOULD GOD'S VIEW ON MARRIAGE AFFECT MY CHOICES?

"The ultimate purpose of marriage is not to make us happy, but to glorify God." —Nancy Leigh DeMoss[10]

Beloved sisters, make no mistake, God's intention for

marriage is to glorify Himself. Please know that the context of this chapter is through the lens of both spouses being believers in Christ, which is vital for relational and spiritual reconciliation. (We are cautioned in 2 Corinthians 6:14-18 to not be unequally yoked. It even speaks of how we are the temple of the living God, which segues so nicely from our previous chapter).

Let's start with the basics.

1. Vows before God are binding (Ecclesiastes 5:4-6 and Numbers 30 to name a few). Most of us had wedding vows on the day we said, "I do." A covenant resulted. Covenants are mentioned over 350 times in Scripture. They're important. They're not just a piece of paper.

2. God wouldn't want anyone to divorce. God embodies perfect love, and His plan is not to harm us. But, because of wicked ways and lustful hearts of men and women, divorce is a very real and scary notion. For further study about divorce, do a short Scripture Sprint: Matthew 5:31-32; 19:1-12; Mark 10:1-12; Luke 16:18; Malachi 2:16; Deuteronomy 24:1-4.

3. God established the special bond of marriage for a reason. The first mention of the word "wife" in our Bibles is in Genesis 2:24 and it refers to becoming *one* flesh. Wives are not autonomous. The passage states the exact opposite: we are one with our husband, by definition, from the beginning of Creation.

Let's expound upon this first glimpse of what a wife

is, because, ladies, I have come to find that it is one of the most noble and God-honoring positions a woman can have. In Genesis 2:18-24, we are called to be helpers. Think that this is a lowly, menial task? Think again! Eve was a suitable helper, created out of man's need. Our husbands need us. No other. The Hebrew term for helper isn't weak or inferior, but rather one of godly worth and strength. God Himself and His Spirit are called "helpers!" Scripture Sprint: Psalm 30:10; 54:4; John 14:26; Hebrews 13:5-6. Now, if that doesn't change your perspective on the vital importance of being a helper, I don't know what will.

Wives are likened to the Church, which Christ laid His life down for! I have to include the entirety of Ephesians 5:22-33, because it paints such a beautiful snapshot of our sacred position:

> Wives, submit to your own husbands, as to the Lord. For the husband is the head of the wife even as Christ is the head of the church, his body, and is himself its Savior. Now as the church submits to Christ, so also wives should submit in everything to their husbands. Husbands, love your wives, as Christ loved the church and gave himself up for her, that he might sanctify her, having cleansed her by the washing of water with the word, so that he might present the church to himself in splendor, without spot or wrinkle or any such thing, that she might be holy and without blemish. In the

same way husbands should love their wives as their own bodies. He who loves his wife loves himself. For no one ever hated his own flesh, but nourishes and cherishes it, just as Christ does the church, because we are members of his body. "Therefore a man shall leave his father and mother and hold fast to his wife, and the two shall become one flesh." This mystery is profound, and I am saying that it refers to Christ and the church. However, let each one of you love his wife as himself, and let the wife see that she respects her husband.

Perhaps you're already familiar with these verses. So, before you gloss over their importance, let's remember truth, which is the engine to the caboose of feelings: the Bible says that the husband is the head of the wife and compares it to Christ being head of the Church (Ephesians 5:23-24). If you flinched at the above verses, sister, it's not because you're ignorant to God's Word or these truths. It's because maybe right now you're thinking, *How is my husband even remotely like Christ (the head)? How can I be the church and love my husband if the church doesn't feel loved?* I've been there.

The solution to that thought is to remain in the context of being the church *first*: adoring Christ, worshipping Christ, submitting to Christ. Subsequently, your role as a wife and his role as the husband will fall into place when you are the Church to Christ first. Sound simple? It is. When we follow

God and His Word, it will never lead us astray. It will lead us to His intended purpose for marriage. And it began in the Garden of Eden.

Everything was perfect before the Fall. I'm sure Eve was happy with Adam and their love abounded. After all, they hadn't sinned yet. She wasn't nagging him. He wasn't harsh with her. Yet, she stumbled and fell the moment she desired more than what God gave and provided freely and lovingly. Don't we all desire more than what we have at times? No wonder the enemy has been using this strategy since the literal beginning of humanity.

With the Fall of man came lawlessness and the need for laws and guidelines to be put in place (as you read previously regarding marriage/divorce).

God wouldn't give us commands if we were completely incapable of following them. Read John 15:9-17. It *is* possible to love our husbands. It is a commandment. Husbands are included in the "one another" phrase—they're not exempt!

If you and your husband are currently at-odds, you may be thinking, *How can I possibly love my husband right now? Forget the witnesses and the covenant, I don't feel like loving him in this moment.*

I can only state the next sentence because I've been in your shoes. It's not that you can't love your spouse; it's that you won't. If you don't see him as anything else right now, please see him as a brother in Christ. Even if you currently see him as your enemy, we're also called to love our enemies (Matthew 5:43-48)! So, no matter how you see your husband today, you're called to love him (John 13:34-35). And, being a matter of the will, it's possible. Having gone through all stages of loving my husband, I can attest to the fact that overcoming the barriers of how they make you feel is possible. You can love him once more. The biggest step was mentioned above: to love Christ *first* and allow Him to reveal His purpose in marital love.

An ongoing step in learning to love your spouse is through your words. Check yourself. If we "slander" our husbands to others, sure, it makes us think we are the right ones and that we have a right to be upset. But, in reality, instead of validation (which only increases bitterness), we are violating our husband's trust and his reputation, which is paramount to him.

How do you speak to your gift from God—your husband? Watch that tongue! Words can seem impossible to tame. Check out the metaphors for the tongue in James 3:1-12:

1. Horses: The bits in their mouths guide them, even their bodies.
2. Ships: How our words steer our life's direction
3. Spark of Fire: Can cause destruction that's difficult to recover from
4. Full of poison: Words that are bitter and resentful will only bring harm. "Resentment is like drinking poison and then hoping it will kill your enemies." -

Nelson Mandela

5. Salt/freshwater: Words can contaminate what should otherwise be pure.
6. Figs on olive trees/grapevine producing figs: It's unnatural for followers of Christ to use words that are detrimental.

Since marriage should be our second most important relationship, one would think it would set the standard of communication to others and model the unity of Christ and the Church. But . . . why do we treat our customers, friends, students, co-workers, etc., with positivity and our spouses with contempt? Why do we forgive others when they wrong us but hold grudges against our spouse? Why do we emotionally and mentally support others but not them? Why do we listen to the voices around us but shut out our husbands and turn a deaf ear toward them?

Pray and ask God to help you. Psalm 141:3, "Set a guard, O Lord, over my mouth; keep watch over the door of my lips!" Search your heart in this moment and *journal* about your thoughts.

Speaking of prayer, it's another great step in learning to love your spouse. Pray specifically for your husband. And not for God to "change" him or teach him a lesson. Lay down your own feelings and pray as his sister in Christ. Pray in the power of Jesus' name to open his eyes, dispel any darkness in his heart, and imbue a spirit of holiness within him.

Realize that he is a treasured image-bearer of God, just like you are. The world tears down your husband enough. Is how you treat him any different than how the world treats him?

One of my favorite steps in loving my husband is to intentionally get to know him. All Love Language types, all Enneagram Types, all MBTI types can fall. The Word of God and His truth is the universal remedy. Knowing your Love Language, Enneagram, and MBTI are simply helpful tools in:

1. Assessing yourself and where you're weak
2. Getting to know your husband
3. Learning how the enemy knows you better than you know yourself

It can give you the equipment you need to know how to combat the enemy and where he targets you. For instance, my Love Language is "Words of Affirmation." I eat those morsels up! How much more so when I'm depraved of words at home did I seek them elsewhere? Well, you know that answer. Here are examples of each of the 5 Love Languages and how they can become entrapped by an EA:

Acts of Service: Maybe the EA cleans your car off at work after it snows.

Giving of Gifts: Maybe the EA brought you coffee when you were running late.

Quality Time: Maybe the EA's intentionality with being near you is a reprieve from the husband who takes time with you for granted.

Physical Touch: Maybe that spark of new physical touch with the EA got you rolling down a hill of longing for more.

Giving examples for Enneagram and MBTI would take extensive time to study and delve into but, take my word for it, these personality tools are helpful in learning how to love your husband.

If you decide to research you and your husband's personality types, please don't take it as Gospel and be consumed with it (I fell into this trap). I can only attest that learning more about myself and the one God chose for me is incredibly helpful in generating compassion, realizing motivations, strengths, weaknesses, stressors, and ways to make amends. If you have a platform like Pinterest, I urge you to start two boards: one for you and one for your spouse. For instance, you could label them: Me–INTP, Type 5, Giving Gifts. Hubby–ESTP, Type 7, Acts of Service, etc. Search for pins that correlate with your personalities and you'll find that it will increase your compassion, not just for him, but for yourself, too.

I pray, ladies, that you were encouraged by this chapter. Realizing the importance of your role as a wife is so critical in acknowledging God's intention for you and your marriage.

A beautiful passage that I recall when thinking about God's design for marriage is Ecclesiastes 4:9-12,

Two are better than one, because they have a good

reward for their toil. For if they fall, one will lift up his fellow. But woe to him who is alone when he falls and has not another to lift him up! Again, if two lie together, they keep warm, but how can one keep warm alone? And though a man might prevail against one who is alone, two will withstand him—a threefold cord is not quickly broken.

Let's continue on our trek to restoring that precious, unique, and sacred bond between you and your husband. And we'll do that by inspecting your own cord first—in surrendered humility.

Humility & Holiness

HOW DO I MAKE THINGS RIGHT WITH GOD?

"The most powerful weapon to conquer the devil is humility. For, as he does not know at all how to employ it, neither does he know how to defend himself from it." —St. Vincent DePaul

By this point, you've recognized your need. You've dealt with fear. You've learned about the battle plan of the enemy, and you've been reminded about God's intention for your life and marriage. You're ready for the next step. And, it's a big one that will change your course forever . . . if you choose to accept it.

Humility is a process. One which we, as humans, can become impatient with. "Tired of the wait?" You see that slogan everywhere, giving us the impression that there's a quicker, more efficient way to do or obtain something. However, we need to stay humble in the wait, knowing that God's timing is perfect regardless of how we feel. If we're too busy complaining about the delay, we're not going to see what God is doing in the meantime. He *is* working.

Israel struggled for 40 years to enter the Promised Land! An entire generation was too busy complaining and being prideful that they never got to see the land that was promised (Deuteronomy 8). Joshua and Caleb were the lone survivors from their generation permitted to enter the Promised Land (see the book of Numbers). It would behoove us to not only learn from Israel and their plight, but to see how God is faithful in His promises, honoring those who humble themselves before Him.

Check out these verses in the holy Word of God that speak to humility and the promises associated with them. Read them all, then choose one or two specific verses to *journal* about. Scripture Sprint: James 4:7-10; 1 Peter 5:6; Matthew 18:1-4; Psalm 25:9-10; 147:6; 149:4, 2 Chronicles 7:14; 33:12-13; Luke 18:14; Proverbs 3:34; Isaiah 66:2; Zephaniah 2:3; Daniel 10:12; Deuteronomy 8:2-6.

As you've no doubt found through these Scriptures, God honors those who choose to humble themselves. Also, that "if" is used a lot. "If" we humble ourselves—it's up to us. The Lord can use testing to see if we will humble ourselves to bring us to our knees and recognize Him as the sovereign God of all Creation. This is no new reality.

Now that you've read about the promises and how God is faithful to those who humble themselves, how do we do that? Below is the biblical flow to reach humility:

Fear of the Lord →   Wisdom→ Humility

"The fear of the Lord is the beginning of wisdom," Psalm 111:10 (also stated in Proverbs 9:10). "Who is wise and understanding among you? Let them show it by their good life, by deeds done in humility that comes from wisdom" (James 3:13, NIV). This, ladies, is our path to humility.

We learned about fearing the Lord in our "Fear & Faith" chapter, and we know that the Lord delivers those who fear Him (Psalm 34:7). But we can't fear the Lord if we don't intimately know Him. Therefore, I implore you to seek Him.

Seeking the Lord is a continuous action and not something we should ever stop doing. As is says in Matthew 7:7, we should ask, seek, and knock. In the Greek, the words used here are for continuous actions. If you read Matthew 7:7, read it again in the context of asking/continuing to ask, seeking/continuing to seek, and knocking/continuing to knock. The intentional Greek word puts it in a whole new perspective, doesn't it?

> Isaiah 55:6-9,
>
> Seek the Lord while He may be found, call upon Him while He is near. Let the wicked forsake his way, and the unrighteous man his thoughts; Let him return to the Lord, and He will have mercy on him; And to our God, for He will abundantly pardon. "For My thoughts are not your thoughts, nor are your ways My ways," says the Lord. "For as the heavens are higher than the earth, so are My ways higher than your ways, and My thoughts than your thoughts."

We usually quote just the last verse, but all the verses together paint the whole canvas of truth. It says to us, "God knows us, therefore, we should repent; because God is sovereign and much wiser than we could ever attempt to be."

The Lord is wise in all ways. Always. To gain healthy fear and wisdom that lead to humility, we need to stay in God's Word and gain wisdom from the Lord.

Why? Because wisdom is better than weapons of war (Ecclesiastes 9:18, 10:10). It's imperative to hone that weapon in order to ultimately sever sin from our lives.

How? James 1:5, "If any of you lacks wisdom, let him ask God, who gives generously to all without reproach, and it will be given him." Also see Psalm 90:12. We need to lean into Him in order for us to know what being upright even means.

Jesus, our perfect example, is a good place to look. Read Philippians 2:1-11.

Now, let's check out some roadblocks to humility. Why? Because God is watching. Because the enemy is waiting.

Roadblock to humility #1: Are you having difficulty taking your eyes off others?

Read Genesis chapter four and take special note on verse seven when God says, "If you do well, will you not be accepted? And if you do not do well, sin is crouching at the door. Its desire is contrary to you, but you must rule over it." There are so many rich instructions in this passage. Cain could only see what he didn't have and what his kin offered. He ignored God's caring words of acceptance. Sister, if you're in that "not good enough" mindset today, remind yourself of how much God loves you—His grace is sufficient for you. Oftentimes, we strive to meet our own expectations or the expectations of others, but we've left God out (this leads to jealousy)! But what does the Lord require of you? Read Deuteronomy 10:12-13 and Micah 6:8. That's it!

He doesn't want you to be like him, or her, or them. He loves you for you. It is crucial to remember that God loves your husband for who he is, too. After all, your husband is also made by God in His image.

Let's talk expectations for a little bit. If we hate when expectations are placed on us or are disgusted with ourselves when we wish we were someone else, why do we place expectations on our husbands and wish they were someone else?

> It is a foolish woman who expects her husband to be to her that which only Jesus Christ Himself can be: ready to forgive, totally understanding, unendingly patient, invariably tender and loving, unfailing in every area, anticipating every need, and making more than adequate provision. Such expectations put a man under an impossible strain. The same goes for the man who expects too much from his wife.
> —Ruth Bell Graham.

Our husbands aren't gods—they're human, just like us. For us to have God-expectations of their mortal selves is like them expecting us to massage their feet and feed them grapes every other hour, while constantly uplifting them. Humanly speaking, it ain't happening! Even more interestingly, do you (at least initially) place the EA on a pedestal, giving him God-like expectations, or go out of your way to care for his needs? Think about that for a long minute.

Now, write down expectations that you have of yourself, of your spouse, and if they're coming from a heart of jealousy or humility. *Journal* about your thoughts and emotions.

I pray you take the path far from Cain's thinking and that you do well. Take heed in the warning that *sin is crouching* at the door. The imagery is much like a lion or a beast, and its desire is for *you*.

Not everything that desires you is to be desired. Something that wants to destroy you *does* desire you; it is sin. Take notice of a different translation, which states that it "lies in wait" at the door. It is patient. Waiting for us to become jealous, bitter, resentful. So, what should we do?

We need to rule over it. In Hebrew, "rule over it" is *mashal*, which means "to master it." Sin is a beast that we need to tame, therefore, we need to be in such control that we can master it.

Roadblock to humility #2: Are you looking too much at yourself?

The opposite of humility, after all, is pride. It's spelled out in Proverbs 11:2, "When pride comes, then comes disgrace, but with the humble is wisdom." Pride has been defined as thinking of ourselves higher than we ought. We need to see ourselves as God sees us: in desperate need of a Savior. Our life is a vapor and our own righteousness apart from God is like filthy rags (James 4:14; Isaiah 64:6).

To expound on this point, read Ecclesiastes 3:18 for wisdom from the wisest mortal to ever live. Solomon relates beasts and humans in birth and death, but it really opened my eyes to something about myself. In the passage, it says that he feels God tests man only to show him that he's a beast. It took time, but I eventually realized that I am capable of beastly behaviors. God humbled me, in part, to show me that I wasn't perfect. He gently revealed to me how simply stubborn, brutal, and sinful I could be. We are all capable of it.

However, there is good news for all who see their sinfulness and humbly repent before the Lord!

Luke 15:11-31 is the well-known story of the prodigal son. He was a child of his father, just like we are children of God. Sometimes, we, like the prodigal, have a rebellious tantrum. It's helpful to know that it wasn't an instantaneous turnaround for the prodigal like, "he left with his inheritance but came right back." No . . . it took time from the point of leaving with his inheritance to the point when he knew full well that he squandered the gift from his father and was humbled. Do you see your husband as a gift from God? How do you treat that gift? Whether you see it today or next month, being involved in an EA is a rebellious act against the Creator of the heavens and the earth, which requires repentance. Breathe.

Let's get back to the story . . . so instead of the son giving up, thinking that his place was destined to be among the pigs, he went back to his father in humility. Just like the son, sometimes we don't feel worthy to be called God's child when we mess up. The Father fully welcomed him back—not as a servant (as the prodigal expected in v. 19) but as a son.

God welcomes us to a place of kinship. Why are we afraid to go back and run to the Father? We need to come to our senses as the son did. God's child is His child, and no one can take us from Him (John 10:28). The way back home was open when the son relinquished his own rebellion against the father.

It's interesting to note that the father didn't stop the son from rebelling (Romans 1 for a real-life correlation) and didn't retaliate or disown his son. He had compassion on him and came *quickly* to him. And sister, I know that God will come quickly to you, as well, if you choose to humble yourself.

Psalm 103:11-19 encompasses everything we just covered. May it be an encouragement to your heart!

Sometimes we want to go our own way like Jonah (Jonah 1:3) or the prodigal son (Luke 15:11-32), but we need to be dependent on the Lord (Jonah 2). We can't run from His presence or hide our sins anyhow (Psalm 139:7-12; Proverbs 28:13-14)!

The choice is up to you: do you want to continue to wallow in the mud with the pigs, or do you realize your need for the love, protection, and promises of your Father? I don't know about you, but I'd prefer the rejoicing of my Father over the empty pride of my choices.

Take this time to inventory your life and your motives (2 Corinthians 13:5). How is your current relationship with your Father? Others? Yourself? Where are your eyes? On yourself? Others? God?

What you've read is humbling and its intent is to bring you to your knees. But . . . that is right where we should be, because that is the place that God can use us.

Remember, *you* are the only one who can wield and use the key of truth in your life story. Ready yourself. Steady yourself. Continue to arm yourself with the Word of God.

Surrendering in obedience is the door to freedom. It sounds like an oxymoron, doesn't it? Much like how God calls us to be servants and how it sets us free (Romans 6:17-22; 1 Peter 2:16). But this is how humility works.

And the time to humble ourselves is now.

In Romans 2 (re-read Romans 1 for context), it describes judgement for all. Bottom line, my friends: God's riches, kindness, forbearance, and patience are for the humble of heart *now*. It is meant to lead us to repentance (Romans 2:4). You have a choice to make. Be humble and allow God to renew your heart and erase sin, sister. Or, continue on the path of pride and see what awaits all who choose it.

Acts 3:19, "Repent therefore, and turn back (*like the prodigal!*), that your sins may be blotted out" (emphasis added). The word, "repent" in Greek (*metanoeo*) means to undergo a change in frame of mind, feeling, and to make a change of principle and practice.

What are some changes you need to make today?

1. In your frame of mind – Am I comparing myself? Am I prideful?
2. Feeling – Do I recognize my need for repentance or is my heart still hard?
3. Change of principle – Am I checking my thoughts,

beliefs, and feelings with the Word of God? What do I need to modify in order to be more in tune with God's principles?

4. Change of practice – What actions should I change to relinquish rebellion?

No one said humility would be easy. There is sacrifice involved to receive blessing.

The "easy-to-say-but-not-to-do" route is to "cut it off" cold turkey, like in Mark 9:43-47. Now, while authors, women speakers, and the like have good intention with biblical backing when saying this, it's easier said than done, isn't it? When I first read that piece of advice in a book for women, I cringed. It seemed a bit callous to me. My thoughts were, *They have no idea what mess I'm in. I can't just cut this or there will be devastating repercussions to me, my marriage, my family, job, reputation . . .* Are your thoughts similar? If so, take a breath.

Let's sharpen our swords and continue the route toward deeper understanding. Our ultimate goal is to cut ties completely (1 Thessalonians 5:22, "Abstain from every form of evil."), but the route to freedom involves examining our hearts in humility first. Read James 4:7-9, and now read verse ten, "Humble yourselves before the Lord, and He will exalt you." There is a promise. There is a purpose. There is a plan. In order to know those promises, purposes, and plans, we must always, always practice humility.

Friends, until I humbled myself, I wasn't ready to cry out to God or confess my wrongdoings. Crying out to God is the essential next step, because friends, I couldn't pray for a way to confess to my husband until I was humbled enough to cry out and confess everything to God. Let's journey on, clinging to the hope and healing that God has in store for you.

Crying Out & Confession

HOW DO I HUMBLE MYSELF?

"To know that God knows everything about me and yet loves me is indeed my ultimate consolation." —R. C. Sproul

In the last chapter, we discussed the "why" of humility. Now, let's dive into the "how." Being humble before the Lord cannot be separate from the two ingredients of crying out and confession. Both are imperative. See an example in Exodus 2:23-25: The Israelites' first step to freedom was to cry out. We need to acknowledge our need for Him *first*.

The psalms are a treasure trove of raw moments of God's servants crying out to Him. One predominant figure, being King David, was mentioned as a man after God's own heart (Acts 13:22).

Let's sit up and pay attention. Take the time now to read

the entirety of Psalm 143. Yes, it's that important! Now, *journal* your raw thoughts about King David actively seeking God and crying out to Him. David and other psalmists knew where their help and consolation came from. Scripture Sprint: Psalm 18:6, 30; 31:14-17; 34:4; 37:39-40; 46:1-2; 91:1-6, 116:1-9; 142; Nahum 1:7.

It's important to know and remind ourselves that our God is a God who shields all who take refuge in Him, because within the 143rd Psalm we read above, verse twelve points out the adversaries of our souls. More than one. In the Hebrew linear, it's spelled out, "those who afflict my soul." To afflict is to cause pain or suffering. Recall the chapter on our true foe and who he can work though.

King David acknowledged to God that he can be weak amidst the attacks of the enemy and called upon Him for strength. Psalm 141:4, "Do not let my heart incline to any evil, to busy myself with wicked deeds in company with men who work iniquity, and let me not eat of their delicacies!" What are the delicacies that your EA entices you with? Freedom? Love? Adventure? Acceptance? Peace? The buffet of tantalizing treats is set by the enemy, and the EA is the maître d'. Turkish delight ring a bell?

Eve didn't spew out the fruit because, quite frankly, it tasted good to her. It was a "delicacy" that she even shared with Adam, causing him to ultimately fall, as well. So, ladies, let's be wise to the fruit and not expect to become wise by it. Meaning, let's fully understand what the fruit's implications are and not believe the enemy's lies about it.

Daughter of God, do you truly see how the EA is afflicting you spiritually? Whether the EA you're involved with is a professing Christian or not, they reside in the enemy's camp to win your heart and cause you to forfeit your marriage: what God joined together (Matthew 19:6; Mark 10:9).

What do those in battle do with adversaries/enemies? Do they eat or drink with them? Do they laugh with them? Do they shower love upon them? Do they give them gifts? Do they join their side? If the soldier is pure in their loyalty to their king and country, then that's a big nope.

We are God's servants. Therefore, when we resolve to serve God with our whole hearts, He will destroy all the adversaries of our souls and will "cut off" our enemies. Do a study on your own sometime of the instances when God's servants cried out to Him in the midst of battle. And we can, too. God will come to our rescue when we cry out to Him in humility with confession.

Consider Psalm 71 and read the entire chapter. You'll find that it is a psalm of dependence upon the Lord for deliverance, and no words of mine could ever compare to the pure and open cry of the psalmist. They knew what Peter knew: that God knows how to rescue the godly from trials (2 Peter 2:9). Humility, in part, is acknowledging that it is God who rescues us—not ourselves. Take solace in knowing that God fights our battles (Ex. 14:14).

We need to hold the sword (read God's Word) and trust

in Him as the psalmist did. Psalm 33:20, "Our soul waits for the Lord; He is our help and our shield." Allow our Help and Shield to really be our help and shield!

Our Help isn't a distant being. He is near to us—the brokenhearted (Psalm 34:18). Jesus, God in the flesh, had *compassion* and *empathy* and *wept* (John 11:33-35). Our precious Lord Jesus knows our weaknesses (Hebrews 4:15). The following verse in Hebrews is so beautiful that I have to write it out. Read it twice and let the comforting truth sink in. Since Christ knows our weaknesses, "Let us therefore come *boldly* unto the throne of grace, that we may obtain *mercy*, and find grace *to help in time of need*" (emphasis added). He does care when we are hurting. We can take solace in knowing that we aren't crying out to a blank wall or empty space of air.

The conduit for crying out and confession is prayer. We know for certain that God hears us. Humanly, we may doubt, but take heart! The following are examples in God's Word that God does hear cries and prayers of the humble and those who submit themselves to His way and authority. Scripture Sprint: 1 Kings 9:3; 2 Kings 19:20; 20:5; Psalm 6:9; 34:15; 65:1-2; 66:17-20; 107; 145:18; 1 John 5:14-15; Proverbs 15:29; Jeremiah 29:11-13; 33:3; Luke 1:13; 18:1-8; Acts 10:31; Hebrews 5:7; Genesis 21:17-18.

Just as God is our shield and refuge, the Spirit is our help when we don't know what to pray, and Jesus is our intercessor: Romans 8:26-27, 34. Even knowing this, if you're like me, I wondered often if I was as heartfelt and focused as I could have been. I feared my connection with Him was clouded, which it had been before humbling myself. I also asked myself if I was praying "enough" with a pure heart and praying for things that would delight God. It's good to humbly check our hearts during prayer.

Even when you fail the Lord, pray (Psalm 51 is an epic prayer of deep confession). Be fully focused during your alone time with God (Matthew 6:6) and don't hide from God. Our natural instinct when we make choices is like Adam and Eve's instinct—to conceal ourselves.

Oftentimes, we seclude ourselves from communion with God or others, but the middle of battle is no time to retreat! As Colossians 4:2 says, we need to be vigilant in prayer; we can't be asleep at our post! Your unit in spiritual battle, which is your family unit, is counting on you to be vigilant. God placed you in your family for a reason.

I realize that the spirit is willing, meaning we *want* to do good and can have good intentions. However, the flesh is weak: depression, exhaustion, sexual desire (it's there!), disease, age. It's a constant battle of thoughts vs. actions: "I should . . . but do I?" The flesh wants to reason away action toward repentance.

Even the Apostle Paul struggled with the battle between the mind and flesh. His story could very well be ours today,

> I find then a law, that, when I would do good, evil
> is present with me. For I delight in the law of God

115

after the inward man: But I see another law in my members, warring against the law of my mind, and bringing me into captivity to the law of sin which is in my members. O wretched man that I am! Who shall deliver me from the body of this death? I thank God through Jesus Christ our Lord. So then with the mind I myself serve the law of God; but with the flesh the law of sin (Romans 7:21-24).

We are not alone in our battle, sisters. Now, read the following verses in Romans 8:1-2, "There is therefore now no condemnation for those who are in Christ Jesus. For the law of the Spirit of life has set you free in Christ Jesus from the law of sin and death." We are free, sisters! Let's live like the battle's won and take off this weight of sin. Are you ready to pour out everything to the Lord?

Confession. We need to be honest about what we are confessing. No sugar-coating. Earlier in this book, we mentioned the "blame game." Do you see yourself as having sinned against God or do you think it's the EA or your husband that needs to repent? Refocus on what God wants from *you*. Recall what God hates and consider the commentary I have along the way.

Proverbs 6:16-20, "There are six things that the Lord hates, seven that are an abomination to Him…:"

1. Haughty eyes (The Hebrew means to exalt something. Are you putting yourself above your husband? Is the church above Christ?)

2. A lying tongue (This one goes without saying. Have you lied recently?)

3. Hands that shed innocent blood (Surely, we haven't committed murder, right? Read Matthew 5:21-22)

4. A heart that devises wicked plans (Have you secretly made plans that would be unloving toward your husband?)

5. Feet that make haste to run to evil (When you're hurt, who do you run to for consolation? Your lawful husband or to the EA?)

6. A false witness who breathes out lies (Are we being truthful witnesses for Christ to all around us?)

7. One who sows discord among brothers (What relationships have been or will be in conflict because of the EA?)

Just like the psalmist was specific in Psalm 120:1-2, "In my distress I called to the Lord, and He answered me. Deliver me, O Lord, from lying lips, from a deceitful tongue," we can be specific and honest with God. If we are not open about our wrongdoings, heed the warnings in the following verses of Proverbs. Hint: it wasn't an accident what the author covered next in his text.

Are you feeling some "tough love" right now? Let me

give you a "hug," because true repentance isn't easy, much like the narrow road. The broad road tells us to sweep our errors under the rug or that it's someone else's fault. This chapter, I've challenged you to look at your own heart, because, friend, I have experienced all the darkness that an EA brings, yet I also had to learn the hard lessons of humbling myself before an Almighty God and lay down my carnal desires and feelings.

Read Hebrews 12:1-2 carefully. Did you notice that it says sin *clings* to us? My father used to run marathons. In practice, weights were tied to his feet so that when the actual race came, he would feel like he could fly and be free of them. Are you trying to run the race of life with the weight of sin still around your ankles? If so, newfound joy and freedom await you if you forgo those hefty weights of sin! 1 John 1:9, "If we confess our sins, He is faithful and just to forgive us our sins and to cleanse us from all unrighteousness." Freedom is a result of falling to our knees in humble prayer and confession before God.

I purposefully didn't have many prompts to journal in this chapter, because I want to encourage you to do something life-changing right now. In your *journal*, write your own song/psalm of confession and cry out to the Lord. Ask the Lord for words to come. Pour out your heart before Him. There is no right or wrong way to do so. It can be a simple two-liner or, as I found it to be, a continual flow from the soul. Take in some fresh air and begin. I'll meet you back here when you've finished.

Welcome back! I pray that the time you spent was a pure and open connection with your loving Creator. In the next chapters, we'll gain more insight from God's Word regarding our spiritual battle. It's time to employ tactics with a healthy tenacity that will bring us to the result.

Tactics & Tenacity

HOW CAN I ACTIVELY CLAIM VICTORY?

"And let us not grow weary of doing good, for in due season we will reap, if we do not give up," Galatians 6:9.

You're probably aware by now that actions toward freedom in Christ are constantly met by ambushes from the enemy. That is why these next chapters are so crucial. The enemy isn't going to allow us safe passage with zero opposition. As we delve into tactics to protect your heart and mind, be tenacious in your efforts! Because, dear friends, the enemy would love nothing more than for you to faint now.

Isolation. Distraction. Escapisms. These are all enemies to your efforts. We can use these unknowingly to divert our minds to cover the reality of our pain. It doesn't take a psychologist with a degree to notice that things like social media, creating busy schedules, excessive phone or TV entertainment, immersing ourselves in our job, being consumed with activities for the kids, and other distractions can come to the same end—the degeneration of relationship between God and spouse. I believe that many EAs can transpire through these life distractions, as well.

When our country was faced with shutdown and some of those distractions were altered, what ensued was increased strain on marriages. Divorce increased[11] and online outlets for EAs, in turn, very likely increased.

To not belabor this point, please just remember that despite the social/economic/cultural climate, if we're spending less time with God in order to cover our wrong choices with distractions, we fool ourselves. When we lose our focus (as Peter took his eyes off Jesus on the water) we begin to slip into waves of darkness. Don't get to a place, ladies, where you're almost suffocating in loss until you cry out to God for rescue. Take these steps now. Be tenacious now.

In one translation of 1 Corinthians 9:25-27, Paul says that he "beats" his body into submission in order to receive the imperishable prize. I don't condone physical harm, of course. I do, however, want you to note the sheer might of his language. I love the definition in the Greek: "discipline by hardships." Another use of the word is "to wear one out." Exercising self-control and suppressing the cravings of the flesh are continuous, rigorous actions.

Galatians 5:16, 25 says, "But I say, *walk* by the Spirit, and you will not gratify the desires of the flesh...If we live by the Spirit, let us also *keep in step* with the Spirit" (emphasis added).

These passages are so rich in wisdom. In the Greek, "walk" is *peripateo*. Since it's an action word, I love to define it as maintaining a certain walk of life and conduct (great Scripture on how to walk: 1 Thessalonians 4:1-8). Plus, it looks like the word "perpetual," doesn't it? The second verse talks about keeping in step, which is literally translated as marching orders for soldiers! We, as God's soldiers, need to follow orders with intentional tenacity. Paul, indeed, set a wonderful example for us.

Many times, we won't feel like spiritually battling against the EA. Paul's body (flesh) wasn't willing, and neither will ours be (Matthew 26:41). We can be met by escapism after escapism until we realize that healing and freedom entails a disciplined act of obedience. Even when we don't feel like it. Even when our flesh fights against us.

Read Acts 9:10-18. When God called Ananias to go meet Saul (Paul), Ananias was afraid. Do you think he wanted to take a detour? Absolutely. Don't be tempted with escapisms to take a detour from what God has called you to do: heal your marriage. Ananias had to go to Straight Street. Remember that verse about God making your path straight (Proverbs 3:6)? Follow Him and He will.

Our part requires obedience despite the fear of the unknown. If we escape battle, we won't know the full extent of God's perfect will unless we trust Him in the unknown. "Understanding can wait. Obedience can't."[12]

God will bless obedience. After all, because of Ananias' obedience, Saul became Paul, who was one of the most revered Apostles of all time. Not to mention, like Paul, we simply must obey and discipline ourselves through the hardships we are enduring.

One biblical avenue to discipline ourselves is through fasting. There are many different types of fasts, and this book will not direct you to one specific fast, as it should be personal and from your heart. A good read when considering fasting is *God's Chosen Fast* by Arthur Wallis. It will walk you through various kinds of fasts and reasons for them. When you seek information about fasting, be sure it's from a reputable Christian site or author. A good guidebook is simply the Word of God.

Other avenues of discipline are in the following sub-chapters: "The Armor of God", "The Fruit of the Spirit", and "The Body of Christ." All are integral to our ultimate freedom in Christ and are part of our battle plan against the enemy of our souls. I realize that these topics may seem elementary to many of you. However, give yourself the grace to read on with new eyes.

Tactics & Tenacity

Part 1 – The Armor of God

"All battles are first won or lost, in the mind." —St. Joan of Arc

Women, we're called to be warriors of light—not just children of light. In 2 Timothy 2, Paul calls Timothy a child, then, later in the text, calls him a soldier for Christ. Let's make that progress today in knowing that we are not only God's child but God's soldier.

We are servants of the King of Light. We represent a Kingdom of Light. We live by a holy set of rules and commands. We wear the armor of light and love (read Romans 13:12-14).

Take a moment to read Ephesians 6:10-20. The powers are otherworldly and so is our armor. We have the amazing blessing to be able to do earthly things to battle our spiritual foe. In reality, this life prepares us for the next. Are you truly equipped? Let's utilize the armory in Ephesians chapter six and start at the top piece of our armor.

The helmet of salvation, interestingly enough, protects the mind. As we talked about in "The True Foe," the mind is often where sin is begotten—where the enemy starts his attack. At the moment of salvation, we put on the certainties of the Word of God in faith. So, start with guarding your mind—surround it with the basic truth of the Gospel that we believed upon. This is our first vital step toward conquering!

Thoughts. They matter.

Ms. Denise Grove, a local women's speaker, did a ladies' talk on January 12, 2016 in my area and spoke on this, which really made me sit up and listen. She told us to take our thoughts "CAPTIVE." Below is an incredibly helpful acrostic (accredited to Ms. Grove) on how to do that:

C – Cease activity (be still)
A – Apply God's Word
P – Press past what you *feel*
T – Talk out loud (cry out!)
I – Invite others in—you were created for community
V – Voice the victory
E – Evaluate for next time

What great advice. I urge you to go through this step-by-step process in your mind each time you're met with thoughts that bring your faith under siege. As I'm sure you've found out, sometimes, as much as we try to keep thoughts captive, we have escapees! It helps me to visualize each thought literally behind bars as I interrogate them.

Since victory or defeat can start in the mind, we need to keep that helmet secure. Our minds are like computers; we don't realize our ability to program them! There's a nifty saying I saw that said, "If you don't program life, it will program you." Since this is an act of the will, be active in programing your mind to follow the will of the Lord, which leads to victory.

The next piece in our supernatural armor is the breastplate of righteousness. We need to protect our hearts from temptation. You never get too old to wear your breastplate. You never outgrow it or become strong enough without it.

I'm sure you know men and women (as I do) who struggled with some form of sexual sin, even after they earn the title of "senior." Emotional/physical/other types of affairs can occur at any moment and at any age or walk of life. That's why we must guard our hearts at all times. Temptation doesn't stop with the young, naïve wife. It lays in wait for the grandmother. The aunt. The deaconess. The mentor. We must strap the breastplate firmly to deflect the fiery darts from landing a bullseye to the chest.

An important, yet small piece of equipment, the belt of truth surrounds the center of our being, supporting the entire body. It's what connects the other pieces together. My favorite part about it? It provides a sword holder. The Word of God needs to be with us at all times, whether we're actively fighting the enemy or at the beach on vacation enjoying the sunshine. Since the enemy can strike anytime, truth needs to be with us at all times.

Next, are the shoes of peace. Shoes naturally help us stand properly and protect our feet from being harmed by obstacles along the way. We're on shaky ground when we seek other ways to have peace other than through God. God's presence *is* peace. If you don't "feel" peace, where do you go to seek it?

For me, it was in the craving of a "deep" relationship . . . the EA. Did the EA bring me peace? I believe, at times, it had the mask of peace. But, when God removed the false mask, it revealed utter turmoil. Conflict lies beneath the surface of unhealthy cravings and ultimately destroys true peace. God showed me that I needed to be the one to create peace within my marital relationship. I knew I couldn't rely on human efforts or relationships to bring me eternal peace. It's up to my intentionality, actions, and thoughts to allow the peace of God to rule over me and my marriage (Philippians 4:6-7).

Now, onto the shield of faith, which is a versatile defensive weapon. We can move it to protect our head, our chest, the middle of our being, and our feet from all fiery darts. Faith says, "No matter what comes my way or from what direction, I believe that God is for me, not against me, and that He has the victory." This thinking thwarts attack attempts aimed at the mind, heart, inner being, and our peace. For exciting verses on how our faith overcomes darkness, read 1 John 5:1-5.

Let's shift our focus to the only offensive weapon mentioned in Ephesians: the Sword (the Word of God). Remember, Jesus used Scripture to defeat the enemy's testing (Matthew 4). Hebrews 4:12 says, "For the Word of God is living and active, sharper than any two-edged sword, piercing to the division of soul and of spirit, of joints and of marrow, and discerning the thoughts and intentions of the heart." It is *the* most effective weapon against the attacks— not our own wavering intentions or half-hearted efforts.

I remember walking through deep woods all alone as the battle of the EA raged in my mind. I wanted to be victorious, but my intention alone, I knew, wouldn't secure triumph. As the leaves rustled all around me in the crisp air, and without a soul in sight, I opened my pocket-sized Bible and began to read Scripture . . . out loud. Tears began to fall as I vocalized the same words to the same psalm over and over again. I see now that that moment was a turning point in my journey to freedom. And you can have a turning point in your journey, as well, if you utilize the perfect offensive weapon (given to us by God Himself!) in your life. Many let their Swords get rusty. May that not be true of you, sister.

Prayer is a piece of our armor that can sometimes be glossed over, but its significance in being paired with the armor is spelled out for us in Ephesians 6:18. It is unfortunately possible, my friend, to be stationary while in our armor. Prayer is the driving force that helps us swing, defend, and actively give the situation, thought, or feeling to God. There is power in prayer that, along with being equipped, will help us in our time of need. What better act can we do than to call upon our Holy King during spiritual battles? We know He will always come to our aid when we are humble before Him.

In this moment, find a quiet place to pray for wisdom. If Jesus found it important to take the time to find a quiet place and pray to His Father, why do we oftentimes think we don't have time for it (Luke 5:16)? When we take initiative to pray, it keeps us from temptation (Luke 22:40).

Now, read Romans 13:12-14 and then come back. The armor itself is light. We are encouraged to "put on the Lord

Jesus Christ." This gives a whole new dimension to intimacy with Christ; He *is* our all-encompassing armor. As children and soldiers of God, we should have confidence knowing that we are property of God (1 Corinthians 6:19-20). The godly woman is sanctified—set apart (1 Peter 2:9-12). We are protected by Him, for Him.

As we close this chapter, know that our armor is personal. No one else can wear your armor for you. You also can't give away your armor to someone else. It's yours to learn how to put on and use effectively in battle.

Even knowing this, we should not disengage from other soldiers in our spiritual battalion. We, as Christians, are fighting the same war, albeit different battles. We need each other.

Tactics & Tenacity

Part 2 – The Body of Christ

"Individualism is not rooted in Scripture." —Rev. Jeff Dunkle

We weren't created to be independent from one another. We were created for community. Christians are like hot coals. When one coal is taken out from among other hot coals, it eventually dies down, becoming cold. We have a relational God who calls us to be relational, so when we have community with one another, it helps the fire continue and spread.

When I was involved in an EA, I wanted to isolate myself and deal with my battle on my own. However, I found that I was more motivated to seek the Lord when I made purposeful plans with God's people. I refocused, was encouraged, and being with the Family of God gave me a fresh confidence to fight the enemy.

Now is not the time to isolate yourself. Chances are, however, that you've already begun or are in the middle of isolation. This makes for a sickly piece of coal.

"Church attendance is as important to the believer as a blood transfusion is to a sick person," D. L. Moody. We go to church for many reasons. One, being that we're bonded by common goals for the Kingdom. Also, we are reminded of Christ's love by others' testimony. Being connected to the Body allows us to serve and focus on others, which helps us to take that huge magnifying glass off ourselves.

Just as the parts of the body can't work independently, we need to stay connected to the Body of Christ. Read Hebrews 3:13. We can be hardened by sin's deceitfulness. Apathetic. Numb. The cure that we find in that verse is that we need encouragement from others and also to encourage others.

Sister, I hope you realize that we need to rise up together and pray for one another so we may stand as one spiritual army for God. One soldier on the battlefield doesn't compare to a horde of soldiers on fire for Christ.

Tactics & Tenacity

Part 3 – The Fruit of the Spirit

"Mountain tops are for views and inspiration, but fruit is grown in the valleys." —Billy Graham

Ladies, these trying times will test your mettle, and you will soon know what you are made of. Life's darkest moments are oftentimes the places where we can exercise our faith and see what fruits we are producing.

What's inside us eventually comes out. If you squeeze an orange, orange juice comes out. When you squeeze a lemon, lemonade comes out.

When I was pressed and squeezed by difficulties during the EA, here's what came out of me: negativity, bitterness, despair, hopelessness, frustration, pessimism, silence, depression, anxiety, exhaustion, sadness, fear . . . self. What manifested was what was inside of me; the results of the root nutrients I surrounded myself with came out in my fruit.

What comes out of you when you're pressed from all sides? Is it the Fruit of the Spirit or some of what I listed above? *Journal* about it. Now, *journal* about what you *want* to come out. To help you with your lists and to see where you're at mentally and emotionally, consider the list on the following page.

Fruit of the Spirit	Antithesis
Love	Hatred
Joy	Sorrow
Peace	Fear
Patience	Impulse
Kindness	Disrespect
Goodness	Cruelty
Faithfulness	Hopelessness
Gentleness	Callousness
Self-Control	Self-Indulgence

You can also check out the list that Paul gave in Galatians 5:19-21 for more specific examples of opposites to the Fruit of the Spirit.

Do you desire to be filled with the fruits of the Spirit? If so, know that it involves yielding, surrendering, and depending upon God. Give it to Him. Rely on His strength.

Why should we be filled?

1. It's commanded (Ephesians 5:18)
2. So Christ's character can be seen in us through endurance, resulting in hope (Romans 5:3-5)
3. Allows us to keep in step with the Spirit (Galatians 5:22-25)
4. So we can serve God joyfully (1 Corinthians 12:4-11)
5. To be able to receive God's teachings (1 John 2:27)

6. To worship God (Ephesians 5:18-19)
7. To experience His guidance (Romans 8:14)
8. To confirm that we are God's child (Romans 8:16-17)
9. So our prayers can be effective (Romans 8:26)
10. So we will refrain from sinful desires (Galatians 5)

The result of being filled with the Spirit is God is being free to accomplish the purpose and plan for which He saved us (Psalm 138:8).

Marrying together the Armor of God with the Body of Christ and the Fruit of the Spirit, be mindful of Colossians 3:12-13, "Put on then, as God's chosen ones, holy and beloved, compassionate hearts, kindness, humility, meekness, and patience, bearing with one another and, if one has a complaint against another, forgiving each other; as the Lord has forgiven you, so you also must forgive." We were forgiven. We are forgiven. What will you do with the forgiveness that was and is given freely to you?

Section 5: The Result

Intro

The culmination of the time we spent soul-searching rests upon these chapters. You may find yourself on the front lines of battle at this point, which is exactly where you are. Steel yourself to press on, sister, because absolutely nothing compares to the freedom and rejoicing that awaits the humble soul!

Forgiveness & Freedom

WHO DO I NEED TO FORGIVE?

"When we hand over every single part of our lives to God in full surrender, we step into freedom." — Caitlin Henderson[13]

In the chapter on confession earlier, we discovered how freedom can be possible when we humbly confess to the Lord and obtain forgiveness. If you've experienced God's forgiveness in your life, you know that it's an unmatched release of all the gunk once held inside. The sense of relief and cleanliness is otherworldly.

Since you know how freeing forgiveness can be, why

withhold it from others? Just as the metaphor Jesus gave of the unforgiving servant (receive a blessing—read Matthew 18:21-35) when the Lord has forgiven us, we should also forgive others (Ephesians 4:32). Not to mention, if we withhold forgiveness from others, it clogs our conduit of prayer (Mark 11:25-26). Who do you need to forgive? If you cringed just now thinking about your husband, that's a sign that forgiveness may be needed there.

You may be negotiating with yourself: *Why would I want to forgive my spouse when I feel neglected and alone?* Oftentimes, we feel alone in our marriage; there's no official poll on this, but I think it's safe to say that loneliness is one of the top reasons why women become involved with EAs.

So, here's a way to combat those feelings: Think of the cross and Christ's sacrifice for you. Now, cross the "l" in "alone" and it becomes "atone." A definition of atone is to make amends. When we repent and make amends with our spouse, we don't have to be in that alone mind frame anymore.

First, we need to forgive them within our hearts for all the reasons mentioned above. If you think you've already forgiven your spouse, let me share with you a telltale sign that you're still holding onto unforgiveness.

As small grievances began to mount once more (after we forgave each other), I found myself overlooking my husband's faults. Doing so was the opposite of exposing them to the EA, which I'd done on occasion in the past, so it was healthy, right? Nope. The proper response should have been to discuss what was upsetting me in a calm, understanding manner with my spouse.

After a long while, I realized I was in "flight" mode and ignoring issues when it came to disagreements. The moment of realization that I was still holding onto unforgiveness came when I had an embarrassing outburst of *fight*. Every grievance I had against my husband spilled out like lava onto him. And I felt horrible afterward. It was in that moment that I realized I was handling my emotions and feelings the wrong way. I hadn't truly forgiven him.

Don't avoid communicating with your husband about how you feel when you feel those emotions. You know him best, so take the time and make sure it's a good time to speak with him. Go to him calmly in a non-accusatory way and see how you can work on those feelings as a couple. It's hard at first, especially if you previously conditioned yourself to hide and hold back your feelings from him. This takes time. Practice identifying your feelings and why you feel those ways. You and your husband are on the same team. Allow him to back you up and hear you out.

Next, consider making amends. This is our end goal, ladies—the final dot on the map to freedom. We are capable, yet not in our own power, of getting our minds off ourselves and purposefully atoning. This is the ultimate act of humility that can set you both free.

When God gave me the clear opportunity to atone with my spouse, He didn't leave me empty. We were at a retreat for couples. Hundreds of people were around when I confessed and pleaded for forgiveness from an open and humble heart. I thank the Lord that He had already prepared the heart of my husband to accept my atonement. I know for a fact that it was the direct result of prayer and humility.

I realize that how it worked for my spouse and I isn't a panacea for all marriages. Your story, of course, will be different. I cannot promise that your husband will have an accepting or forgiving heart.

That is why you must first and foremost humble yourself. And pray for your spouse and for your own heart. Pray for discernment and for the words that you speak to come from the Holy Spirit that is powerful within you. Our God is a God of miracles.

If you're looking for a great way to take steps in forgiveness and toward an outward apology, check out the "7 A's" from the "Resolving Everyday Conflict" series by Peacemaker Ministries. You can find them in a blog mentioned in the endnotes.[14]

The bottom line is this: When you forgive others, Christ will pour His blessing upon you and forgive you (Matthew 6:14-15; Luke 6:37).

Keep a tender heart toward your spouse and *journal* about battles your husband might be facing today and write a prayer of forgiveness. Perspective is paramount when you desire to plant the precious seed of compassion and understanding. It blooms into healing and restoration.

There may be one more person who you need to inwardly forgive: the person involved in the EA. By this point, you may have pent up anger and resentment toward the EA. I caution you: Don't seek revenge. Easier said than done, isn't it? Even though we are charged to forgive, our human nature wants revenge for the damage the EA caused (yes, damage was also caused by our own hands, and I'm not negating that). EAs can cause pain emotionally, physically, mentally, socially, relationally, and spiritually. It's not a natural thing to instantly forgive what has been done to us or by us. May these verses comfort you today and help ease that bent to seek revenge: 1 Samuel 24:21; Proverbs 24:17-18; Romans 12:17-19. Put the EA at the Lord's feet and leave him there. Sever what is driving the wedge in your marriage.

Once all has been forgiven and your conscience is clear before God and others, the finish line is close by. And what a beautiful, freeing, joyful finish line it is.

Restoration & Rejoicing

WHAT AWAITS ME IF I FOLLOW GOD INSTEAD OF
MY HEART?

"(Love) does not rejoice at wrongdoing, but rejoices with the truth," 1 Corinthians 13:6

This is the breath we've been holding. This is the moment we've been praying for.

Hebrews 10:35-36, "Therefore, do not throw away your confidence, which has great reward. For you have need of endurance, so that when you have done the will of God you may receive what is promised."

My dear sister, restoration is possible, and rejoicing can come from the darkest nights of mourning. May you have peace knowing that it can take time to get to that place. John 14:27, "Peace I leave with you; my peace I give to you. Not as the world gives do I give to you. Let not your hearts be troubled, neither let them be afraid." This is a promise from our beloved Jesus. Be at peace, friend!

Consider a mature forest teeming with life, the trees tall and sturdy. Now, consider how quickly it can be cut or burned down. Further yet, consider how much longer it would take to re-plant and re-grow that forest to its original state.

On average, it would take 50 years to regrow that forest, whereas burning it or cutting it down would take a fraction of that time. Ladies, maybe the forest of your marriage was burnt down instantly or cut down significantly over the years, and you don't see the hope. Do you believe that the One who created heaven and earth can restore your marriage? I do.

In His timing and in His way.

Sometimes, it's not what we imagined the healing would look like. Regardless of whether our marriage was instantly healed or if it's going to take many years to rebuild, God is faithful. Give it time and give it to God; lay your marriage at the feet of His throne. We need to be faithful to Him in the waiting. Do you have a humble and willing heart to accept that God's timing and methodology differs from ours?

God can make beauty from ashes, and that's what we need to cling to. Isaiah 61:1-3 sums all of this up by saying,

> The Spirit of the Lord God is upon Me, because the Lord has anointed Me to preach good tidings to the poor; He has sent Me to heal the brokenhearted, to proclaim liberty to the captives, and the opening of the prison to those who are bound; to proclaim the acceptable year of the Lord, and the day of vengeance of our God; To comfort all who mourn, to console those who mourn in Zion, to give them *beauty for ashes*, the oil of joy for mourning, the garment of praise for the spirit of heaviness; That they may be called trees of righteousness, the planting of the Lord, that He may be glorified (emphasis added).

This is a prophecy of Jesus Christ (Jesus recited it to proclaim who He was in Luke chapter four). Jesus is stating plainly who He came for: the poor, brokenhearted, captives, the bound, mourners . . . you and me, sister.

May we be planted of the Lord and come forth as trees of righteousness for His glory! Hold fast and be rooted in Christ and in the Word of God. Our God is a God of restoration, forgiveness, and healing. *Journal* about these truths and add Scripture you've found that support these truths.

During our time together, I pray that you realized that truth will set you free (John 8:31-36). God put instructions in place to allow us to enjoy the benefits of fellowship with Him. When we follow His commands, we are able to enjoy all the benefits of fellowship with Him. That, after all, is the greatest treasure at the end of this journey.

Jesus is coming back. Are you at peace? 2 Peter 3:8-14. We have eternal glory to look forward to. When Christ comes back for us, will you be confident in how you dealt with the apple?

"Blessed is the man who remains steadfast under trial, for when he has stood the test he will receive the crown of life, which God has promised to those who love Him." James 1:12.

Yes, this journey has been difficult. However, it's not new news that we must go through many trials to enter the Kingdom of God (Acts. 14:22), but when we are tested, may we come forth as gold (Job 23:10).

"For I consider that the sufferings of this present time are not worth comparing with the glory that is to be revealed to us." Paul is saying in Romans 8:18 that it hasn't been revealed yet; the best is yet to come, my friend!

I don't know about you, but I can't wait to see my Heavenly Father with His open arms greeting me and rejoicing over me, much like the father of the prodigal son. We aren't the only ones who rejoice when we gain victory over a sin that so easily entices us. Our Heavenly Father rejoices, too. Read Zephaniah 3:17.

As we close, check yourself. Are you . . .
- ☐ Humble before the Lord
- ☐ Praying without ceasing
- ☐ Trusting without limits
- ☐ Patient in the waiting
- ☐ Thankful in heart, not just words
- ☐ Content in all circumstances
- ☐ Serving the Lord

For the grace of God has appeared, bringing salvation for all people, training us to renounce ungodliness and worldly passions, and to live self-controlled, upright, and godly lives in the present age, waiting for our blessed hope, the appearing of the glory of our great God and Savior Jesus Christ, who gave himself for us to redeem us from all lawlessness and to purify for himself a people for his own possession who are zealous for good works (Titus 2:11-14).

Don't give up the good fight, Warrior Wife. Keep battling the enemy of your soul with humility, steadfastness, and prayer. Remember our time together. Remember the One who loves you so deeply that He sacrificed for you in order to set you free.

> *Dearest Father,*
>
> *I pray that through this arduous journey out of the clutches of the enemy and into Your loving arms that Your daughter will rise up from the ashes and claim victory over the emotional attachment in her life. I pray that she has found solace in Your Word, Your promises, and in Your truth. May she be set free from bondage, according to Your will, and may her life be a living testimony of Your goodness and grace. May she see the need of those around her who are perishing, so that she may shine her precious light for all to see. May Your face shine upon the institute of marriage as Your daughter seeks to restore what was broken. Give her courage, faithfulness, and favor. In your Son's matchless name I pray, amen.*

Section 6: The Really Rough Questions

Intro

Though the overall war against the enemy of our souls is the same, our individual battles can look either different or similar. In this segment, I wanted to cover some specific common battles women may have. Be encouraged as we walk through these hard questions together.

WHAT IF I'M ALSO DEALING WITH DEPRESSION/ANXIETY?

"When I understand that everything happening to me is to make me more Christlike, it resolves a great deal of anxiety."
—A. W. Tozer

This is an area I am well acquainted with. When my son was born, I developed post-partum depression thanks to ever-evolving hormones. This depression stuck with me for many years. Depression melded into anxieties, and suddenly, I was left coping with both. Medication became a normalcy for my life. I felt like a lab rat, offered multiple medications to see which one would be the "right fit." Don't get me wrong, medications are necessary in many cases, and I wouldn't try to disprove anyone's positive results. For me, however, I had to realize that much of the depression and anxiety came from discontentment in my marriage and family life. It's natural that when discontentment in your marriage is present, discontentment in all aspects of life follows.

Reality had slaughtered my expectations and *that* is a tough pill for anyone to swallow. For the four total years that I was involved in EAs, I realized that it took a major toll on my mental, emotional, spiritual, and physical state. But I was in denial all those years. With taking medications and believing that I needed them to feel better (and not repent), it was hard on my actual biological mental state. I was causing literal brain damage because of the EAs' illusions (there are countless studies on how depression/anxiety affects the mind). Initially, my depression was clinical/hormonal. Over time, it became circumstantial/hormonal (because those hormones won't leave us alone!). It also manifested itself in visible ways. I drastically lost weight, I was irritable, apathetic, isolated myself, I had brain fog and a complete lack of motivation (among other symptoms).

I did what I could in the moment—downloaded mood apps and tracked my feelings on charts and tried to implement self-care and created a colorful graph for ways to motivate myself. I took vitamins, ate better, took time to rest . . . all for nothing. I knew the answer, and I tried to mask it for many years.

After I humbled myself and my marriage was restored by God's mercy, I made the personal decision to cease medications. I saw my mood apps go from months of logging deep blue depression to logging orange-colored happy states instantly.

As odd as it sounds, my depression thrust me into the loving arms of the Savior. Just as Charles H. Spurgeon puts it, "Sometimes in deep depression, in the midst of the darkest shadows, Christ appears and seems sweeter than He ever was before. When all the created streams have run dry, then the everlasting fountain bubbles up with a pure and cooling stream." I pray you'll find comfort in those words today if you're dealing with dark caverns of depression in your heart and mind.

Your depression journey is unique, however, the effects of it are universal. Depression has been defined as, "the result of trying to find satisfaction in something or someone other than God." I found out how true that was and how I was trying to numb my pain in the wrong ways.

Sins are burdens on our backs that we carry, which can be misdiagnosed as depression. It also manifests itself in physical ways, causing health problems. Even King David felt depression's weight. Re-read the chapter on Psalm 143 as a refresher! Furthermore, these verses of Psalm 32:3-4 really make it real:

"For when I kept silent, my bones wasted away through my groaning all day long. For day and night Your hand was heavy upon me; my strength was dried up as by the heat of summer." Wow. Sure sounds like a crystal clear description of depression, doesn't it? Even centuries old, this verse still resonates.

Now, read how it was overcome in Psalm 32:1-7 and *journal* about your findings.

It's comforting to know that a "man after God's own heart" felt what we feel and was able to continue to write about the goodness of the Lord. What a classic case of God turning beauty from ashes! David's story isn't unique and is also true for many other heroes of the faith, as you know.

If you're still not sure how to combat depression, allow me to share a personal experience with you so that we can walk through this together.

It was mid-day. I had zero energy. If anyone could have negative motivation (worse than zero motivation!), I did. I was prepared to sleep another few hours in my dimly-lit room and just drift into nothingness when I cried out to God in my mind: "I can't do this. I don't want to do this. Save me." All of a sudden, God drove me to use my fingers to type on my phone keyboard to search for a Bible-based preacher. I clicked on a video sermon and closed my eyes. Little did I know that the sermon was a call to action for soldiers of Christ. That compelled me to rise from my bed with fresh eyes.

Try searching for solid Bible-based sermons. Note: Do

your research on these preachers/worship leaders first and make sure they're not those false prophets we talked about. Your spirit will stir within you when you hear something that disagrees with the inherent Word and true love of God.

Music is also an amazing way to lift our spirits to the throne of God while the battle rages. Worship in the waiting is healing. So, if you're a music person (or even if you're not), I recommend that you listen to positive and truth-filled worship music.

God chose me to climb the mountains of depression and anxiety, knowing my struggle, but also knowing the victory that I would have over them through Him. I realize now that a purpose was to show others how those mountains don't have to be obstacles but opportunities to show God's glory.

This chapter can be summed up by more words from Charles H. Spurgeon (yes, he just might be my favorite preacher!), "Often depression of spirit and great misery of soul are removed as soon as we quit our idols and bow ourselves to obedience before the living God. We must do this with all our hearts and all our souls, and then our captivity will end."

The similarities between the Israelites, Egypt, Pharaoh, and our journey from the apple's captivity are uncanny. Egypt for the freed Israelites represented the old life . . . old patterns . . . slavery. There is a pharaoh in your life not willing to give you up. Is it depression? Anxiety? Whatever it is, the pharaoh tests your resolve and shows you your chains. Often. Those chains can be internal but also manifest externally, as I mentioned previously.

Pharaoh tried to bargain with the Israelites, offering for them to "obey God" while staying in Egypt, partially following the Lord, excluding others, and bringing less than what was necessary to the altar.

But God wanted His people to *go . . . leave . . . be cut off from . . .* without compromise. God wants the same from us today, because He knows how liberating it will be (read Colossians 3:5-10).

Do you long for your captivity in the dank dungeon of depression to be over? Follow the prescription in Psalm 31: acknowledge your sin to the Lord, pray to the Lord, and believe in your heart and mind that He is our help amidst trouble. Sometimes, God chooses to not heal us completely from depression or anxiety. If it lingers, humble yourself and ask God what He is trying to show you or do through you.

"When the cares of my heart are many, Your consolations cheer my soul." Psalm 94:19.

"Humble yourselves, therefore, under the mighty hand of God so that at the proper time He may exalt you, casting all your anxieties on Him, because He cares for you." 1 Peter 5:6-7. Our suffering is temporary (v. 10). It's also comforting to know that while we may have anxiety, we are never alone (Hebrews 13:5b). I pray you've found some encouragement and helpful advice in this chapter.

WHAT IF IT'S NOT WITH A GUY?

"No matter what colors you try to paint your choices over with, sin is always the color of darkest night." —Rachel D. Lyne

Despite the aversion of this notion for some of you, this chapter is completely relevant to the times in which we live. We live in an era where there is a target on God's rock-solid truth and commands of love and marriage. We're bombarded with mixed messages in our culture and it's only appropriate to address battles that may be very real for some of you. Sin isn't exclusive and neither are the methods the enemy uses. The bottom line: God's truth can't and won't be changed by man's laws or by our feelings. Again . . . God's truth cannot and will not be changed by man's laws or by our feelings.

First, if you're reading this, I want you to know that we all have life battles, and some battles look different than others. If you're attracted to a woman today, know that this isn't a foreign or new battle for women.

This battle begins in the mind. As with any battle in the mind, little by little, thoughts, fantasized pictures, lifestyles, and desires overtake someone until they cave under the pressure of their own thoughts. Anyone can falsely believe the world's voices, which over time, become louder than God's. If we're not actively protected by the Armor of God, we're even more susceptible to fall for this ploy of the enemy.

We need to call the thoughts for what they are: spiritual battles.

We need to call falling for a girl or guy other than your spouse exactly what it is: sin.

Otherwise, you'll be met by compromise after compromise.

You don't need a theology, philosophy, or religion degree to understand God's Word on this point. Yet, so many are duped into believing a different gospel than the one that was written. The facts are clear in God's Word.

Argument 1: "The word 'homosexual' isn't in the Bible." Let's do some digging that doesn't require a thesis. We know the word "homosexual" wasn't in existence until 1906. The King James Version of the Bible dates back to the year 1611. Think about that. Nearly 300 years after the KJV was published, a word was created for the meaning. Naturally, the exact word wasn't in the first English language version!

Let's look in the Bible at texts that describe homosexuality, spelling it out for us. Here is one specific passage that can't be argued no matter how anyone wants to spin it.

In Romans 1:21-28, Paul wrote:
For although they knew God, they did not honor him as God or give thanks to him, but they became futile in their thinking, and their foolish hearts were darkened. Claiming to be wise, they became fools, and exchanged the glory of the immortal God

for images resembling mortal man and birds and animals and creeping things. Therefore, God gave them up in the lusts of their hearts to impurity, to the dishonoring of their bodies among themselves, because they exchanged the truth about God for a lie and worshiped and served the creature rather than the Creator, who is blessed forever! Amen. For this reason, God gave them up to dishonorable passions. For their women exchanged natural relations for those that are contrary to nature; and the men likewise gave up natural relations with women and were consumed with passion for one another (*this is the definition of homosexuality*), men committing shameless acts with men and receiving in themselves the due penalty for their error. And since they did not see fit to acknowledge God, God gave them up to a debased mind to do what ought not to be done (clarification added).

I included the context instead of just the one verse about women, because it's important to see humanity's progression and see the definition of homosexuality in plain sight, even without the exact word being used in the text. Even Paul in the first century knew about the battle of women being attracted to one another. Also, I challenge you to do a Scripture Sprint: Leviticus 18:22; 20:13, Deuteronomy 23:17, 1 Kings 14:24 (male temple or cult prostitutes and sodomites all have the same root–homosexuality), 1 Corinthians 6:9-10 and 1 Timothy 1:8-11. *Journal* about what you find. The concept and reality of homosexuality transcends both Old and New Testaments, contrary to popular belief. Burning for one another is a result of putting the created above the Creator. Sexual immorality was a common sin all throughout Scripture. Don't let it be so with you, sister!

Circling back to the passage, Paul said they worshiped their own wisdom and the things of the world. Wait . . . isn't that why Eve ate the fruit from the tree of the knowledge of good and evil? She wanted to be like God in His knowledge. I see a theme here . . .

Argument #2: "What matters is my happiness." Much like Eve's battle, we tend to think that we are the only ones in the middle of the battlefield and our happiness is what matters regardless of what God or others think.

Despite what society shoves down our throats and what our sin nature begs for, we aren't the center of it all. This life isn't about seeing what exotic or erotic things we can discover about ourselves or about trying new things to see if they'll make us happy. Quote that line to the world and they'd rip it to shreds. Because the world wants you to believe that the path you're on is your own personal, enlightening discovery. The world wants you to think that achieving what makes you feel good is the end goal, even if that means cutting ties with your spouse, other Christians, and ultimately . . . your Creator. That is the world's desire for you. And it's easy to fall into.

In this moment, if you're struggling with affections for another woman, be blunt and honest with God. For perspective and a bird's eye view of the battlefield, ask Him to show you what pain would be in store for the ones you love if you continue on the path of lusting after women. Deep down, sister, you know what God intends for you and your marriage. Moreover, since God has already revealed what awaits those who blatantly reject Him and His ways, ask Him to remind you of it.

Self-indulgence is easy for us humans. I understand it can feel unnatural to seek after what God intends. The road leading away from self-indulgence is the more difficult road to follow and requires much effort and focused thought (Scripture Sprint: 1 Peter 4:12-13,16; James 1:25; Philippians 1:29; 2 Timothy 2:3). God never said the right choice or path would be easy.

It's much easier to take the broad road (Matthew 7:13). However, I encourage you to take the more difficult road: the one of true repentance. If you are still set on staying on the path of self-indulgence, you will leave a path of destruction in your wake. Is a brief moment of what the world calls "happiness" worth the pain of others and the grief of the Holy Spirit? Or, is everlasting joy in Christ what you truly seek?

Argument #3: "God is only and all about love." What a deep rabbit trail this one is! But, I am elated to share with you findings from the Word of God that demonstrate how He is love (pure, sinless love) and still is Judge and holy.

Some may argue that homosexual-type sins are only written about in the law of the Old Testament and were abolished when Jesus came. Well, we disproved that with the previous argument, but read Matthew 5:17-20.

Now, how do we do that? Romans 8:3-5.

Next, read Romans 13:8-10, James 2:8, and Galatians 5:13-20. These passages can be where the world likes to twist it to their own agenda. Yes, of course, it tells us to love. But not in a love defined by the world. The kind of love that Jesus calls us to is not *eros* (sexual); it is not lust. The kind of love He displays and wants us to emulate is esteeming one another above ourselves, having generous concern for, being faithful to (Greek word *agape*). Is adultery putting our spouse above ourselves? Is having relations that bind our heart and/or body to another woman being faithful to our husbands? You know the answers. And, hopefully, by this time, you understand that having relations with another woman is unloving to our God who set marriage, order, time and space, authority, guidelines to live by, and love itself in place.

In perspective, note that 1 John 4:8 uses the *agape/agapao* version of love: "Anyone who does not love does not know God, because God is love."

Argument #4: "Jesus never spoke against homosexuality." Oh? Matthew 19:4,

He (Jesus) answered, "Have you not read that He who

created them from the beginning made them male and female, and said, 'Therefore a man shall leave his father and his mother and hold fast to his wife, and the two shall become one flesh?' So they are no longer two but one flesh. What therefore God has joined together, let not man separate."

The Lord Jesus Christ did not express any other way to be joined in marriage.

If you claim to be a Christian today, you know that Jesus is fully God and fully man. Jesus was here at the beginning of time (read Colossians 1, especially vv. 15-20). No wonder Jesus quoted the words from Genesis. He was there. He created marriage. He would know how it's done.

Listen closely, friend. I believe that God created man in His image. Therefore, I do not hate or condemn those who choose the homosexual lifestyle—it is not my place nor my heart. God is the ultimate judge in matters of the heart, and I am merely a servant who desires to proclaim His truth. I don't attend marches. I don't wish harm on anyone. I do, however, hope that all see the truth of the Word of God for themselves before it's too late. The enemy has had millennia to perfect his disguise of "love" to the world. That is exactly why we need to pore over the Scriptures. Diligently study and follow them. The natural result in doing so is God opening your eyes wide to His holy and perfect love. It will steer you far from wrong, no matter what form it takes.

Check your heart. If you have affections for another woman, are you apathetic towards the consequences? Ask yourself why. *Journal* it and be honest with yourself. Sometimes it's not as simple as just thinking or feeling apathetic. Maybe a situation happened to you in the past that scarred you. Maybe your heart is hard against your husband. Maybe you didn't get much of a college life and want to explore. Maybe you're on medication that alters the way you view the world. Maybe a diagnosis catapulted you to "live life to the fullest." Whatever the deep reasoning is, I guarantee you that once the root of your curiosity is found out and dealt with in biblical and healthy ways, you'll realize that the curiosity was simply the whispers of the enemy who meets you at every fork in the road.

WHY IS THIS HAPPENING TO ME . . . *AGAIN*?

"You may have to fight a battle more than once to win it."
—Margaret Thatcher

Whether Margaret was referring to politics or policies, what matters is that it rings true in the spiritual realm, as well. Sometimes we can fall back into what enticed us to begin with, whether with the same person or not. Times are constantly changing, and it's foolish for us to think that it couldn't happen to us again. After all, the enemy knows where we are vulnerable.

If you're stuck in a second EA, instead of the selfish response, "how could I be so blind," ask God what He wants to show you through your unique situation.

For me, my heart was not humble enough the first time to really give the glory to God. "Repentance" the first time was hollow and half-hearted. I slowed the pace of my spiritual growth and didn't hone my defenses for a possible second attack. Like the fool I was, I challenged the enemy in my head saying, "That will never happen to me again." Well, it did. The enemy took it as a challenge accepted. I am not at all proud to have had a second EA, but I am deeply thankful to the Lord for what He showed me through it. I'm thankful for the pain that brought me to my knees.

True humility came when destruction came crashing down and I could do nothing of my own to stop the carnage upon my mind, body, and soul. I had finally realized I could do nothing apart from God (John 15:5). I genuinely cried out for mercy and deliverance from the only One who could deliver.

After your first EA, perhaps your marriage began to slip into old patterns, causing you to dwell on how things used to be with the first EA. Those thoughts can trigger when the mercy of God is forgotten and when difficulties are faced once more in marriage. It can be pleasing to remember the "good" times in Egypt (the old life) when we are hurting in our marriage, can't it? However, remember the folly of the Israelites who grumbled to Moses (Exodus 14:11-12,16:2-3, Numbers 11:1, 20:3-5, and many more!). More than once, they complained that they had delicacies/safety in Egypt even though they had been enslaved! They glamorized their past because of present discomfort and didn't mention the beatings, ceaseless work, and lack of freedom in Egypt. The old life, full of false peace and false pleasure, has nothing good to offer. Allow it to pass away (2 Corinthians 5:17).

But just as the Israelites complained on more than one occasion, so do we. We have good times in our marriage where godly praise flows from our lips. Other times, tensions rise, communication dwindles, and we're left feeling alone and neglected once more. My sister, this is no cause to remember the past and wish for it back—the times when we feel like complaining are exactly the times when we need to humble ourselves, praise the Lord, and seek biblical ways to heal our marriage (prayer, the Word, counseling, reading Christian marriage books, etc.).

Remembering only "good" times will cause you to romanticize the evil that surrounded the situation. Ladies, when you look back at Egypt like the Israelites (Exodus 16:2-3), when you look back like Lot's wife (Genesis 19:26), when you look back with longing to the place that God delivered you *from*, there will be consequences.

If the enemy tempts you to look back, it's a prime opportunity to remind him of his future. And . . . to remember our future, as well (2 Corinthians 5 and so many more).

If the past still nags, remember the pain of the EA. Remember the confusion. Remember the cage. Remember the shame. There is a healthy type of disdain for the past, which catapults us into the forgiving arms of Jesus every time. When we direct our thoughts on the truth and God's deliverance, we shall not be deceived by the delicacies of evil (Jeremiah 4:14, Philippians 4:7-8). As you are to run from the serpent, run also from those the enemy sends your way. Pray for discernment. Listen to the "Spirit Stirs." And let God battle.

In the Gospels (Matthew 26), Jesus told Peter that he would deny Him three times before the rooster crowed. Peter vehemently disagreed; there was no way he would do that! Yet, it was as Jesus said. There is a beautiful aspect to this passage that can speak to your heart today. Even though Peter denied knowing Jesus three times, God still gave Peter a purpose and a new direction in ministry. He became the rock upon which the church was built. There is still hope for you.

Even after a victory is won, there are still battles to face in the future. As long as we breathe this earthly air, we are bound to experience heartache among other difficulties: loss of a job, illness, heartache, death of a loved one. Circumstances are the recipes that brew harmful feelings, which, when the "cooking time" is just right, produce actions contrary to God's intended will for our lives.

May this verse not ring true for you: 2 Peter 2:22, "What the true proverb says has happened to them: 'The dog returns to its own vomit, and the sow, after washing herself, returns to wallow in the mire.'"

My dear sister, if you are trapped in a second EA today and you have cried out to God for repentance but God seems silent, consider this: true repentance cannot be obtained unless we also give our husbands a heartfelt chance. If God gave/gives you a way through repentance, shouldn't you give your husband a chance at that freeing, glorious turn-around, too? Say this out loud, "God didn't give up on me. Therefore, I won't give up on my husband." Take time right now and *journal* about the feelings you had when you stated that sentence.

Recognizing the humanity of our spouse and realizing that they also face battles will give us a healthier perspective and helps guard our own hearts. Re-read the chapters in "The Result" to further awaken your heart to your spouse.

WHAT IF IT ALMOST OR DID GO INTO THE PHYSICAL REALM?

"Since we have these promises, beloved, let us cleanse ourselves from every defilement of body and spirit, bringing holiness to completion in the fear of God," (2 Corinthians 7:1).

Our minds are powerful. Imagination, when left unbridled, takes us to scary and forbidden places we never dreamed we would be or wanted to be. More often than not, if our minds traveled to physical realms, our bodies are not far behind.

If you and the EA have exchanged physical relations but have not had intercourse, still beware. See Romans 6:12-14, especially verse three. We struggle immensely when we use our parts as "instruments" of sin. We convince ourselves that if we just give a small part, but not the whole part, that we are safe. Sometimes we call it "cheating" and not a full-blown "affair." Because, my sister, we reason with ourselves that in an affair there are biblical grounds for divorce if reconciliation is not sought by your husband. So, it's not the same thing . . . right?

This is a gray area in our minds while we are in sin, but when confronted with reality, we have to remember that sin is sin in all its various forms.

Let's get right into the Word. Jesus' Sermon on the Mount is most famous for the Beatitudes. However, it takes

161

a dark turn as Jesus warns about lust (which He parallels to adultery) in Matthew 5:27-28. In the very next verses, it talks about those instruments of sin. Read the following verses in Matthew 5:29-30.

Wow. Well, *that* passage isn't in the forefront of preaching these days, is it? Jesus may be quite literal while scholars believe He is being metaphorical. I would never tell anyone to chop off a body part, so please don't. But, I do want you to see that Jesus in this passage is aggressively passionate about the implications of lust and using our body for sin. It's no wonder that the following verses yet (Matthew 5:31-32) speak of that lust/adultery resulting in divorce. This is the dangerous and deadly slope, my sisters. Jesus was quite deliberate in stating what He did in the order He did. It starts in the mind, then the body, then defilement resulting in ultimate loss.

Take note of Paul's words in 1 Corinthians 6:13, "The body is not meant for sexual immorality, but for the Lord, and the Lord for the body." It's no wonder that defilement of the body grieves the Lord so deeply. We are *His*. Read the remainder of 1 Corinthians chapter six to get a full picture of God and what He intends for your body. *Journal* about your findings and feelings.

To further define the cheating vs. affair argument, in all fairness, your husband may think cheating is synonymous with an affair. Consider if what you did would be done to you. You'd feel tremendous pain from an emotional affair as you would from a physical affair on different levels, but with the same overwhelming feelings of betrayal.

This book's mission is to help guide you, with the Lord's help, far away from the ledge of having any type of affair or unhealthy emotional attachment and to help you navigate out of the specific intricacies of those forbidden fruit.

In instances when a physical affair has occurred or cheating has been defined as an affair by your spouse, please seek a Christian counselor for help.

Biblically, there can be forgiveness and healing after a physical affair (reconciliation). It takes two willing hearts, the Word, and good counsel to continue in the journey of marriage. But, before that, your heart has to reach some truths. Read John 8:1-11 and Luke 7:36-50 and *journal* your thoughts. Jesus cautioned the woman in John to "sin no more." In Luke, he told the woman to "go in peace." Peace is attainable once more. God still has great blessings and plans for *you*. Don't forget that, dear sister! When you humble yourself, take the stand to sin no more, and hold fast to it; there can be forgiveness and lasting peace.

Still not convinced? There are countless reliable Christian resources available encompassing the aftermath, effects, and healing from a physical affair. I encourage you, sister, to seek them out. For a continuing physical affair, I urge you to seek intensive Christian professional marital counseling.

Having a Christian counselor vs. a counselor who does not acknowledge God is key. It's simple: the non-Christian counselor can guide you only as well as the world itself could guide you (1 Corinthians 3:19-20). I urge you to pursue God's will for your life through His Word and the wisdom of a licensed counselor/pastor who will point you to the cross and lead your thoughts heavenward.

Surround yourself with other Christian wives and those who have walked the path you are on. Find a women's support group near you. We are commanded to carry each other's burdens and you don't have to do it alone (Galatians 6:2). Your story, like mine, may be the key to unlocking a sister's prison cell.

HOW DO I COPE WITH KIDS?

"Each day of our lives we make deposits in the memory banks of our children." —Chuck Swindoll

Our life's story, whether we are aware of it or not, is always teaching and molding future generations. Children (and not just your own!) are watching you and how you live . . . very closely. Your life is their blueprint, even though they are the ultimate architects of their choices.

You're probably already aware of this fact, and it may even be the reason why you hold a copy of this book in your hands. Because you know they are watching, listening, and mimicking.

As a mother of two, I also had to come to this awareness and it brought much guilt. How do you deal with that guilt?

One step toward dissolving that guilt is to remind yourself that our Heavenly Father understands what it's like to be a parent. You may think thoughts like, "Well, Jesus never had kids . . . how can He relate?"

No surprisingly, Jesus *does* relate to parenthood even though He didn't have biological (in our worldly sense) children. Jesus Christ and God the Father are one (John 10:30) and have been from the beginning (John 1:1-3). Throughout the Old Testament and New Testament, God cared for, "pulled His hair out" about, prayed for, fed, got angry with, loved, listened, helped, cried over, comforted, related to, understood, protected, provided for, wanted the best for, taught, had patience with, and desired trust and respect from . . . His children. Convicting stuff!

But yes, of course, our Father is perfect. And we are not. That is why we must allow God to work and heal within and through us to become what He intended us to be for our children. Holding onto guilt and shame keeps us in a cage. That cage keeps us from relating to and loving our children freely. You can be vulnerable with them.

I'm not telling you to shout all your shortcomings from the rooftops. I'm simply saying that you can admit to your children that you aren't perfect. You can tell them you fell. You can confess that you've had wrong thoughts or actions.

The key is to include what the Lord has done despite your shortcomings. You can admit to them that you couldn't do it without God's direction. You can tell them He helped you get back up. You can confess that you needed God's forgiveness. In showing your children (no matter the age) that we are human and fail sometimes, it gives opportunity to also show them God's mercy and grace in a real way. When they inevitably make poor choices, I pray that they will remember how the Lord came to your aid, knowing that there is forgiveness and healing in Jesus Christ. What a beautiful way to turn guilt into a teachable blessing to glorify the Lord! The most important thing I can do as a mother to raise a godly generation is to be a godly example. *Journal* about your thoughts.

In Closing

I hope you've found in *The Apple* a practical, immediate help in your time of desperate need for healing. The words within this book were entwined to weave a tapestry of faith that women can relate to in this day and age. I pray that you are able to claim victory over the sin that so easily entangles us women by listening to the voice of God in prayer and reading His Word to bring you to the ultimate redemption for yourself and your marriage. Stay strong, Warrior Wives and Women. Know that I am praying for your situation to be turned into something good for the Kingdom of Christ (Genesis 50:20). Don't let the enemy win. Keep fighting. You are loved. Thank you so much for coming.

My Journal for the Journey

Date: __/__/__

Thoughts on What I Read:

_____

_____

_____

_____

_____

Prayer to My Creator:

_____

_____

_____

_____

_____

How I Feel:
(Words or Drawings):

Battle Plan:
(Personal Goal Toward Freedom in Christ):

_____

_____

_____

_____

_____

_____

_____

My Journal for the Journey

Date: __ / __ / __

Thoughts on What I Read:

_____

_____

_____

_____

_____

Prayer to My Creator:

_____

_____

_____

_____

_____

How I Feel:
(Words or Drawings):

Battle Plan:
(Personal Goal Toward Freedom in Christ):

_____

_____

_____

_____

_____

_____

My Journal for the Journey

Date: __/__/__

Thoughts on What I Read:

_____

_____

_____

_____

_____

Prayer to My Creator:

_____

_____

_____

_____

_____

How I Feel:
(Words or Drawings):

Battle Plan:
(Personal Goal Toward Freedom in Christ):

_____

_____

_____

_____

_____

_____

My Journal for the Journey

Date: __/__/__

Thoughts on What I Read:

_____

_____

_____

_____

_____

Prayer to My Creator:

_____

_____

_____

_____

_____

How I Feel:
(Words or Drawings):

Battle Plan:
(Personal Goal Toward Freedom in Christ):

_____

_____

_____

_____

_____

_____

_____

My Journal for the Journey

Date: __/__/__

Thoughts on What I Read:

_____

_____

_____

_____

_____

Prayer to My Creator:

_____

_____

_____

_____

_____

How I Feel:
(Words or Drawings):

Battle Plan:
(Personal Goal Toward Freedom in Christ):

_____

_____

_____

_____

_____

_____

_____

My Journal for the Journey

Date: __ / __ / __

Thoughts on What I Read:

_____

_____

_____

_____

_____

Prayer to My Creator:

_____

_____

_____

_____

_____

How I Feel:
(Words or Drawings):

Battle Plan:
(Personal Goal Toward Freedom in Christ):

_____

_____

_____

_____

_____

_____

_____

My Journal for the Journey

Date: __/__/__

Thoughts on What I Read:

_____

_____

_____

_____

_____

Prayer to My Creator:

_____

_____

_____

_____

_____

How I Feel:
(Words or Drawings):

Battle Plan:
(Personal Goal Toward Freedom in Christ):

_____

_____

_____

_____

_____

_____

My Journal for the Journey

Date: __/__/__

Thoughts on What I Read:

_____

_____

_____

_____

_____

Prayer to My Creator:

_____

_____

_____

_____

_____

How I Feel:
(Words or Drawings):

Battle Plan:
(Personal Goal Toward Freedom in Christ):

_____

_____

_____

_____

_____

_____

My Journal for the Journey

Date: __/__/__

Thoughts on What I Read:

_____

_____

_____

_____

_____

Prayer to My Creator:

_____

_____

_____

_____

_____

How I Feel:
(Words or Drawings):

Battle Plan:
(Personal Goal Toward Freedom in Christ):

_____

_____

_____

_____

_____

_____

_____

My Journal for the Journey

Date: __/__/__

Thoughts on What I Read:

_____

_____

_____

_____

_____

Prayer to My Creator:

_____

_____

_____

_____

_____

How I Feel:
(Words or Drawings):

Battle Plan:
(Personal Goal Toward Freedom in Christ):

_____

_____

_____

_____

_____

_____

My Journal for the Journey

Date: __/__/__

Thoughts on What I Read:

_____

_____

_____

_____

_____

Prayer to My Creator:

_____

_____

_____

_____

_____

How I Feel:
(Words or Drawings):

Battle Plan:
(Personal Goal Toward Freedom in Christ):

_____

_____

_____

_____

_____

_____

My Journal for the Journey

Date: __/__/__

Thoughts on What I Read:

_____

_____

_____

_____

_____

Prayer to My Creator:

_____

_____

_____

_____

_____

How I Feel:
(Words or Drawings):

Battle Plan:
(Personal Goal Toward Freedom in Christ):

_____

_____

_____

_____

_____

_____

My Journal for the Journey

Date: __/__/__

Thoughts on What I Read:

_____

_____

_____

_____

_____

Prayer to My Creator:

_____

_____

_____

_____

_____

How I Feel:
(Words or Drawings):

Battle Plan:
(Personal Goal Toward Freedom in Christ):

_____

_____

_____

_____

_____

_____

My Journal for the Journey

Date: __ / __ / __

Thoughts on What I Read:

_____

_____

_____

_____

_____

Prayer to My Creator:

_____

_____

_____

_____

_____

How I Feel:
(Words or Drawings):

Battle Plan:
(Personal Goal Toward Freedom in Christ):

_____

_____

_____

_____

_____

_____

_____

My Journal for the Journey

Date: __/__/__

Thoughts on What I Read:

_____

_____

_____

_____

_____

Prayer to My Creator:

_____

_____

_____

_____

_____

How I Feel:
(Words or Drawings):

Battle Plan:
(Personal Goal Toward Freedom in Christ):

_____

_____

_____

_____

_____

_____

_____

My Journal for the Journey

Date: __/__/__

Thoughts on What I Read:

_____

_____

_____

_____

_____

Prayer to My Creator:

_____

_____

_____

_____

_____

How I Feel:
(Words or Drawings):

Battle Plan:
(Personal Goal Toward Freedom in Christ):

_____

_____

_____

_____

_____

_____

_____

My Journal for the Journey

Date: __/__/__

Thoughts on What I Read:

_____

_____

_____

_____

_____

Prayer to My Creator:

_____

_____

_____

_____

_____

How I Feel:
(Words or Drawings):

Battle Plan:
(Personal Goal Toward Freedom in Christ):

_____

_____

_____

_____

_____

_____

My Journal for the Journey

Date: __ / __ / __

Thoughts on What I Read:

_____

_____

_____

_____

_____

Prayer to My Creator:

_____

_____

_____

_____

_____

How I Feel:
(Words or Drawings):

Battle Plan:
(Personal Goal Toward Freedom in Christ):

_____

_____

_____

_____

_____

_____

My Journal for the Journey

Date: __/__/__

Thoughts on What I Read:

_____

_____

_____

_____

_____

Prayer to My Creator:

_____

_____

_____

_____

_____

How I Feel:
(Words or Drawings):

Battle Plan:
(Personal Goal Toward Freedom in Christ):

_____

_____

_____

_____

_____

_____

_____

My Journal for the Journey

Date: __ / __ / __

Thoughts on What I Read:

_____

_____

_____

_____

_____

Prayer to My Creator:

_____

_____

_____

_____

_____

How I Feel:
(Words or Drawings):

Battle Plan:
(Personal Goal Toward Freedom in Christ):

_____

_____

_____

_____

_____

_____

My Journal for the Journey

Date: __/__/__

Thoughts on What I Read:

_____

_____

_____

_____

_____

Prayer to My Creator:

_____

_____

_____

_____

_____

How I Feel:
(Words or Drawings):

Battle Plan:
(Personal Goal Toward Freedom in Christ):

_____

_____

_____

_____

_____

_____

My Journal for the Journey

Date: __/__/__

Thoughts on What I Read:

_____

_____

_____

_____

_____

Prayer to My Creator:

_____

_____

_____

_____

_____

How I Feel:
(Words or Drawings):

Battle Plan:
(Personal Goal Toward Freedom in Christ):

_____

_____

_____

_____

_____

_____

My Journal for the Journey

Date: __ / __ / __

Thoughts on What I Read:

_____

_____

_____

_____

_____

Prayer to My Creator:

_____

_____

_____

_____

_____

How I Feel:
(Words or Drawings):

Battle Plan:
(Personal Goal Toward Freedom in Christ):

_____

_____

_____

_____

_____

_____

_____

My Journal for the Journey

Date: __/__/__

Thoughts on What I Read:

_____

_____

_____

_____

_____

Prayer to My Creator:

_____

_____

_____

_____

_____

How I Feel:
(Words or Drawings):

Battle Plan:
(Personal Goal Toward Freedom in Christ):

_____

_____

_____

_____

_____

_____

My Journal for the Journey

Date: __/__/__

Thoughts on What I Read:

_____

_____

_____

_____

_____

Prayer to My Creator:

_____

_____

_____

_____

_____

How I Feel:
(Words or Drawings):

Battle Plan:
(Personal Goal Toward Freedom in Christ):

_____

_____

_____

_____

_____

_____

_____

My Journal for the Journey

Date: __ / __ / __

Thoughts on What I Read:

_____

_____

_____

_____

_____

Prayer to My Creator:

_____

_____

_____

_____

_____

How I Feel:
(Words or Drawings):

Battle Plan:
(Personal Goal Toward Freedom in Christ):

_____

_____

_____

_____

_____

_____

My Journal for the Journey

Date: __/__/__

Thoughts on What I Read:

_____

_____

_____

_____

_____

Prayer to My Creator:

_____

_____

_____

_____

_____

How I Feel:
(Words or Drawings):

Battle Plan:
(Personal Goal Toward Freedom in Christ):

_____

_____

_____

_____

_____

_____

My Journal for the Journey

Date: __ / __ / __

Thoughts on What I Read:

_____

_____

_____

_____

_____

Prayer to My Creator:

_____

_____

_____

_____

_____

How I Feel:
(Words or Drawings):

Battle Plan:
(Personal Goal Toward Freedom in Christ):

_____

_____

_____

_____

_____

_____

_____

My Journal for the Journey

Date: __/__/__

Thoughts on What I Read:

_____

_____

_____

_____

_____

Prayer to My Creator:

_____

_____

_____

_____

_____

How I Feel:
(Words or Drawings):

Battle Plan:
(Personal Goal Toward Freedom in Christ):

_____

_____

_____

_____

_____

_____

My Journal for the Journey

Date: __ / __ / __

Thoughts on What I Read:

_____

_____

_____

_____

_____

Prayer to My Creator:

_____

_____

_____

_____

_____

How I Feel:
(Words or Drawings):

Battle Plan:
(Personal Goal Toward Freedom in Christ):

_____

_____

_____

_____

_____

_____

_____

My Journal for the Journey

Date: __/__/__

Thoughts on What I Read:

_____

_____

_____

_____

_____

Prayer to My Creator:

_____

_____

_____

_____

_____

How I Feel:
(Words or Drawings):

Battle Plan:
(Personal Goal Toward Freedom in Christ):

_____

_____

_____

_____

_____

_____

My Journal for the Journey

Date: __/__/__

Thoughts on What I Read:

_____

_____

_____

_____

_____

Prayer to My Creator:

_____

_____

_____

_____

_____

How I Feel:
(Words or Drawings):

Battle Plan:
(Personal Goal Toward Freedom in Christ):

_____

_____

_____

_____

_____

_____

My Journal for the Journey

Date: __/__/__

Thoughts on What I Read:

_____

_____

_____

_____

_____

Prayer to My Creator:

_____

_____

_____

_____

How I Feel:
(Words or Drawings):

Battle Plan:
(Personal Goal Toward Freedom in Christ):

_____

_____

_____

_____

_____

_____

My Journal for the Journey

Date: __ / __ / __

Thoughts on What I Read:

_____

_____

_____

_____

_____

Prayer to My Creator:

_____

_____

_____

_____

_____

How I Feel:
(Words or Drawings):

Battle Plan:
(Personal Goal Toward Freedom in Christ):

_____

_____

_____

_____

_____

_____

My Journal for the Journey

Date: __/__/__

Thoughts on What I Read:

_____

_____

_____

_____

_____

Prayer to My Creator:

_____

_____

_____

_____

_____

How I Feel:
(Words or Drawings):

Battle Plan:
(Personal Goal Toward Freedom in Christ):

_____

_____

_____

_____

_____

_____

My Journal for the Journey

Date: __ / __ / __

Thoughts on What I Read:

_____

_____

_____

_____

_____

Prayer to My Creator:

_____

_____

_____

_____

_____

How I Feel:
(Words or Drawings):

Battle Plan:
(Personal Goal Toward Freedom in Christ):

_____

_____

_____

_____

_____

_____

My Journal for the Journey

Date: __/__/__

Thoughts on What I Read:

_____

_____

_____

_____

_____

Prayer to My Creator:

_____

_____

_____

_____

_____

How I Feel:
(Words or Drawings):

Battle Plan:
(Personal Goal Toward Freedom in Christ):

_____

_____

_____

_____

_____

_____

_____

My Journal for the Journey

Date: __ / __ / __

Thoughts on What I Read:

_____

_____

_____

_____

_____

Prayer to My Creator:

_____

_____

_____

_____

_____

How I Feel:
(Words or Drawings):

Battle Plan:
(Personal Goal Toward Freedom in Christ):

_____

_____

_____

_____

_____

_____

My Journal for the Journey

Date: __/__/__

Thoughts on What I Read:

_____

_____

_____

_____

_____

Prayer to My Creator:

_____

_____

_____

_____

_____

How I Feel:
(Words or Drawings):

Battle Plan:
(Personal Goal Toward Freedom in Christ):

_____

_____

_____

_____

_____

_____

_____

My Journal for the Journey

Date: __ / __ / __

Thoughts on What I Read:

_____

_____

_____

_____

_____

Prayer to My Creator:

_____

_____

_____

_____

_____

How I Feel:
(Words or Drawings):

Battle Plan:
(Personal Goal Toward Freedom in Christ):

_____

_____

_____

_____

_____

_____

Endnotes

1. Keller, Timothy. *Facebook*, November 1, 2016. https://www.facebook.com/TimKellerNYC/posts/the-sin-that-is-most-destructive-in-your-life-right-now-is-the-one-you-are-most-/1286940228012527/.

2. Statista. "Global digital population as of October 2020." January 27, 2021. https://www.statista.com/statistics/617136/digital-population-worldwide/#:~:text=Almost%204.66%20billion%20people%20were,percent%20of%20total%20internet%20users.

3. Furtick, Steven (Elevation Church). "When Anxiety Attacks." *YouTube*. October 17, 2016. https://www.youtube.com/watch?v=dMpzvw4yhB8.

4. Boa, Kenneth. *Conformed to His Image: Biblical and Practical Approaches to Spiritual Formation* (Grand Rapids: Zondervan, 2001), 348.

5. MacArthur, John. *The Gospel According to Jesus* (Zondervan, published in association with the literary agency of Wolgemuth & Associates, Inc., 2008), 142.

6. Lexico n.d. "keyword: obsess." Accessed February 1, 2021. https://www.lexico.com/definition/obsession.

7. Ingram, Chip, ed. *The Daily Walk Bible* (Carol Stream, IL: Tyndale House Publishers, Inc., 2017),

1159.

8. McDowell, Josh. "Helping Your Kids to Say No," Focus on the Family, October 16, 1987.

9. Chalmers, Thomas, and William Hanna, eds. *The Expulsive Power of a New Affection* (Minneapolis, Minnesota: Curiosmith, 2012), 27.

10. DeMoss, Nancy Leigh. *Lies Women Believe: And the Truth that Sets Them Free* (ed. Moody Publishers, 2007), ISBN: 9780802479532.

11. Brownwell, Taylor, "Divorce Rates and COVID-19," *The National Law Review*, October 16, 2020, https://www.natlawreview.com/article/divorce-rates-and-covid-19.

12. Ingram, Chip, ed. *The Daily Walk Bible* (Carol Stream, IL: Tyndale House Publishers, Inc., 2017), 277.

13. Henderson, Caitlin. *Instagram* @ faithfamilyandfarming. Theel, Stephanie. *Pinterest* "Maiden in Waiting."

14. Taylor, Justin, "The Seven A's of Confession." *The Gospel Coalition,* January 15, 2010, https://www.thegospelcoalition.org/blogs/justin-taylor/the-seven-as-of-confession/.

About the Author

Mrs. Rachel Gehman (pen name Rachel D. Lyne) is an emerging author with TBN's Trilogy Christian Publishing, Inc. and is thrilled to debut her first of many inspiring works. Rachel is a Christian Living blogger, poet, singer/songwriter/pianist and artist. A church administrative professional for fourteen years and former worship leader of nine years, Rachel desires to know God and make Him known. Marrying her passion of words and heart to share the Good News, her focus is to come alongside others in their unique spiritual journey to offer inspiration and renew hope. You can visit her online at racheldlyne.com, Facebook at "Rachel D. Lyne, Author," and on Instagram (@racheldlyne). Rachel lives with her husband of fifteen years and two children in Pennsylvania where they serve in various ministries at a local church.

CPSIA information can be obtained
at www.ICGtesting.com
Printed in the USA
BVHW040000200921
616975BV00001B/4